LEVEL 8 Suppleme

CW00336532

ANSWER BOOK

ULTIMATE
MUSIC THEORY

By Glory St. Germain ARCT RMT MYCC UMTC &
Shelagh McKibbon-U'Ren RMT UMTC

The LEVEL 8 Supplemental Workbook is designed to be
completed with the Advanced Rudiments Workbook.

GSG MUSIC

Enriching Lives Through Music Education

ISBN: 978-1-927641-59-0

The Ultimate Music Theory™ Program

The Ultimate Music Theory™ Program lays the foundation of music theory education.

The focus of the Ultimate Music Theory Program is to simplify complex concepts and show the relativity of these concepts with practical application. This program is designed to help teachers and students discover the excitement and benefits of a sound music theory education.

The Ultimate Music Theory Program is based on a proven approach to the study of music theory that follows the *"must have"* Learning Principles to develop effective learning for all learning styles.

The Ultimate Music Theory™ Program and Supplemental Workbooks help students prepare for nationally recognized theory examinations including the Royal Conservatory of Music.

GSG MUSIC

Library and Archives Canada Cataloguing in Publication
UMT Supplemental Series / Glory St. Germain and Shelagh McKibbon-U'Ren

Gloryland Publishing - UMT Supplemental Workbook and Answer Book Series:

GP-SPL	ISBN: 978-1-927641-41-5	UMT Supplemental Prep Level
GP-SL1	ISBN: 978-1-927641-42-2	UMT Supplemental Level 1
GP-SL2	ISBN: 978-1-927641-43-9	UMT Supplemental Level 2
GP-SL3	ISBN: 978-1-927641-44-6	UMT Supplemental Level 3
GP-SL4	ISBN: 978-1-927641-45-3	UMT Supplemental Level 4
GP-SL5	ISBN: 978-1-927641-46-0	UMT Supplemental Level 5
GP-SL6	ISBN: 978-1-927641-47-7	UMT Supplemental Level 6
GP-SL7	ISBN: 978-1-927641-48-4	UMT Supplemental Level 7
GP-SL8	ISBN: 978-1-927641-49-1	UMT Supplemental Level 8
GP-SCL	ISBN: 978-1-927641-50-7	UMT Supplemental Complete Level
GP-SPLA	ISBN: 978-1-927641-51-4	UMT Supplemental Prep Level Answer Book
GP-SL1A	ISBN: 978-1-927641-52-1	UMT Supplemental Level 1 Answer Book
GP-SL2A	ISBN: 978-1-927641-53-8	UMT Supplemental Level 2 Answer Book
GP-SL3A	ISBN: 978-1-927641-54-5	UMT Supplemental Level 3 Answer Book
GP-SL4A	ISBN: 978-1-927641-55-2	UMT Supplemental Level 4 Answer Book
GP-SL5A	ISBN: 978-1-927641-56-9	UMT Supplemental Level 5 Answer Book
GP-SL6A	ISBN: 978-1-927641-57-6	UMT Supplemental Level 6 Answer Book
GP-SL7A	ISBN: 978-1-927641-58-3	UMT Supplemental Level 7 Answer Book
GP-SL8A	ISBN: 978-1-927641-59-0	UMT Supplemental Level 8 Answer Book
GP-SCLA	ISBN: 978-1-927641-60-6	UMT Supplemental Complete Level Answer Book

* Resources - An annotated list is available at UltimateMusicTheory.com under Free Resources.

Ultimate Music Theory

LEVEL 8 Supplemental

Table of Contents

Score: 60 - 69 Pass; **70 - 79** Honors; **80 - 89** First Class Honors; **90 - 100** First Class Honors with Distinction

Ultimate Music Theory: *The Way to Score Success!*

Workbooks, Exams, Answers, Online Courses, App & More!

A Proven Step-by-Step System to Learn Theory Faster - from Beginner to Advanced.

Innovative techniques designed to develop a complete understanding of music theory, to enhance sight reading, ear training, creativity, composition and musical expression.

All UMT Series have matching Answer Books!

The UMT Rudiments Series - Beginner A, Beginner B, Beginner C, Prep 1, Prep 2, Basic, Intermediate, Advanced & Complete (All-In-One)

♪ 12 Lessons, Review Tests, and a Final Exam to develop confidence
♪ Music Theory Guide & Chart for fast and easy reference of theory concepts
♪ 80 Flashcards for fun drills to dramatically increase retention & comprehension

Rudiments Exam Series - Preparatory, Basic, Intermediate & Advanced

♪ 8 Exams plus UMT Tips on How to Score 100% on Theory Exams

Each Rudiments Workbook correlates to a Supplemental Workbook.

The UMT Supplemental Series - Prep Level, Level 1, Level 2, Level 3, Level 4, Level 5, Level 6, Level 7, Level 8 & Complete (All-In-One) Level

♪ Form & Analysis and Music History - Composers, Eras & Musical Styles
♪ Melody Writing using ICE - Imagine, Compose & Explore
♪ 12 Lessons, Review Tests, Final Exam and 80 Flashcards for quick study

Supplemental Exam Series - Level 5, Level 6, Level 7 & Level 8

♪ 8 Exams to successfully prepare for nationally recognized Theory Exams

UMT Online Courses, Music Theory App & More

♪ UMT Certification Course, Teachers Membership & Elite Educator Program
♪ Ultimate Music Theory App correlates to the Rudiments Workbooks
♪ Free Resources - Teachers Guide, Music Theory Blogs, videos & downloads

Go To: UltimateMusicTheory.com

At Ultimate Music Theory we are passionate about helping teachers and students experience the joy of teaching and learning music by creating the most effective music theory materials on the planet!

Introducing the Ultimate Music Theory Family!

Meet So-La! So-La loves to sing and dance.

She is expressive, creative and loves to tell stories through music!

So-La feels music in her heart. She loves to teach, compose and perform.

Meet Ti-Do! Ti-Do loves to count and march.

He is rhythmic, consistent and loves the rules of music theory!

Ti-Do feels music in his hands and feet. He loves to analyze, share tips and conduct.

So-La & Ti-Do will guide you through Mastering Music Theory!

Enriching Lives Through Music Education

The Ultimate Music Theory™ Comparison Chart to the 2016 Royal Conservatory of Music Theory Syllabus.
Level 8

The Ultimate Music Theory™ Rudiments Workbooks, Supplemental Workbooks and Exams prepare students for successful completion of the Royal Conservatory of Music Theory Levels.

UMT Advanced Rudiments Workbook plus the LEVEL 8 Supplemental Workbook = RCM Theory Level 8.
♫ Note: Additional completion of the UMT LEVELS 4 - 7 Supplemental Workbooks are strongly suggested.

RCM Level 8 Theory Concept	Ultimate Music Theory Advanced Workbook
Required Keys - Major and minor keys up to seven sharps and flats	**Keys Covered** - Major and minor keys up to seven sharps and flats

Pitch and Notation
 	
- Alto and tenor clefs (notes and Key Signatures)
 	
- Score types: string quartet and modern vocal in short and open score
 	
- Transcription of a melody to any other clef at the same pitch (including alto and tenor clefs)
 	
- Transposition of a melody to concert pitch for orchestral instruments:
   - in B flat (trumpet, clarinet)
   - in F (French horn, English horn)
	Pitch and Notation Covered
	
	- Alto and Tenor Clefs (notes and Key Signatures)
	
	- Score Types - String Quartet Score and Modern Vocal Score in short (condensed/close) score and in open score
	
	- Rewriting a melody at the same pitch in a different clef (including alto and tenor clefs)
	
	- Transposition of a melody to Concert Pitch for:
	   - Orchestral B flat Instruments (Trumpet and Clarinet)
	   - Orchestral F Instruments (English horn and French horn)

Scales - All major and minor (natural, harmonic, and melodic) scales in treble, bass, alto or tenor clefs, starting on any scale degree (using key signatures and/or accidentals) - Diatonic modes: Ionian (major), Dorian, Phrygian, Lydian, Mixolydian, Aeolian (natural minor), and Locrian, starting on any pitch (using key signatures and/or accidentals)	**Scales Covered** - All Major and minor (natural, harmonic and melodic) scales in the Treble, Bass, Alto or Tenor Clefs, starting on any scale degree (using Key Signatures and/or accidentals) - Chromatic (Harmonic and Melodic), Octatonic, Pentatonic (Major and minor), Blues and Whole Tone scales - Modes: Ionian (Major), Dorian, Phrygian, Lydian, Mixolydian, Aeolian (natural minor) and Locrian, starting on any pitch and written using Key Signatures and/or accidentals
Chords and Harmony - Triads built on any degree of a major or minor (natural or harmonic) scale in root position and inversions using functional chord symbols and root/quality chord symbols - Dominant 7th chords and their inversions using functional chord symbols and root/quality chord symbols - Leading-tone diminished 7th chords in minor keys using functional chord symbols and root/quality chord symbols - Identification and writing of authentic, half, and plagal (IV-I or iv-i) cadences on a grand staff, employing root position triads in major and minor keys, in keyboard style and chorale style - Identification of cluster chords, quartal chords, and polychords	**Chords and Harmony Covered** - Triads in Open and Close Position (in root position and inversions) - Triads built on any scale degree of the Major and harmonic minor scales, in root position and inversions, using Functional Chord Symbols * Workbook Pages - Review of Functional Chord Symbols and Root/Quality Chord Symbols for triads built on any degree of a Major or minor (natural or harmonic) scale in root position and inversions - Dominant 7th Chords in Open and Close Position (in root position and inversions) using Functional Chord Symbols * Workbook Pages - Review of Functional Chord Symbols and Root/Quality Chord Symbols for Dominant 7th Chords (in root position and inversions) - Diminished 7th Chords in minor keys using Functional Chord Symbols * Workbook Pages - Review of Functional Chord Symbols and Root/Quality Chord Symbols for Leading-Tone Diminished 7th Chords in minor keys (root position only) * Workbook Pages - Review of Identification and writing of Authentic, Half, and Plagal (IV-I or iv-i) Cadences on a Grand Staff, employing root position triads in Major and minor keys, in Keyboard Style * Workbook Pages - Identification and writing of all Cadences in Chorale Style - Identification of Triads (Major, minor, Augmented or diminished), Seventh Chords, Cluster Chords, Quartal Chord and Polychords

RCM Level 8 Theory Concept (Continued)

Rhythm and Meter
- Hybrid meters (such as 5/4, 7/8 and 10/16)
- Application of time signatures, bar lines, notes, and rests

Intervals
- All simple and compound intervals (and their inversions) up to a fifteenth above or below a given note (using key signatures or accidentals)

Melody and Composition
- Melodic passing tones (unaccented) and neighbor tones (unaccented), within a harmonic context of I, IV, V chords (major keys) and i, iv, V (minor keys)
- Composition of a contrasting period in a major or minor key, given the first two measures

Form and Analysis
- Identification of any concept from this level and previous levels within a short music example
- Application of functional or root/quality chord symbols to a melody, using root-position I, IV, and V chords (major keys) or i, iv and V chords (minor keys), maintaining a clearly defined harmonic rhythm
- Identification of types of motion: parallel, similar, contrary, oblique, and static

Music Terms and Signs
- Tempo, Dynamics and Articulation

Music History/Appreciation
Guided Listening: "Ordo Virtutum" by Hildegard von Bingen (Scene 4: Quae es, aut unde venis?). Listening Focus: plainchant, monophonic texture

Guided Listening: "Sumer Is Icumen In" ("Reading Rota") - Anonymous, 13th Century. Listening Focus: canon, ostinato, polyphonic texture

Guided Listening: "El grillo" by Josquin des Prez. Listening Focus: frottola, word painting

Guided Listening: "Kaboran (Gamelan Prawa)" - the Javanese gamelan. Listening Focus: gamelan, metallophones

Guided Listening: "Evening Raga: Bhopali" - the raga in Indian music. Listening Focus: raga, tala, sitar

Examination
Level 8 Theory Examination

Ultimate Music Theory Advanced Workbook (Continued)

Rhythm and Meter Covered
- Hybrid Duple, Hybrid Triple and Hybrid Quadruple Time
- Application of Time Signatures, Bar Lines, notes and rests in Simple, Compound and Hybrid Time

Intervals Covered
- All simple and compound intervals (and their inversions) up to a fifteenth above or below a given note (using key signatures or accidentals)

Melody and Composition Covered
* Workbook Pages - Melodic Passing Tones (unaccented) and Neighbor Tones (unaccented) within a harmonic context of I, IV, and V chords (Major keys) or i, iv and V chords (minor keys)
* Workbook Pages - Composition of a contrasting period in a Major or minor key, given the first two measures

Form and Analysis Covered
* Workbook Pages - Identification Review of any concept from this level and previous levels within a short music example
* Workbook Pages - Application of functional or root/quality chord symbols to a melody, using root-position I, IV, and V chords (Major keys) or i, iv and V chords (minor keys), maintaining a clearly defined harmonic rhythm
* Workbook Pages - Identification of types of motion: parallel, similar, contrary, oblique, and static

Music Terms and Signs Covered
- Tempo, Dynamics and Articulation

Music History/Appreciation Covered
* Workbook Pages - Life and Music of Hildegard von Bingen; "Ordo Virtutum, Scene 4: Quae es, aut unde venis?" by Hildegard von Bingen. Listening Focus: Plainchant, Monophonic Texture
Free Resources for Listening Activities & Watching Videos
* Workbook Pages - "Sumer Is Icumen In" ("Reading Rota") - Anonymous, 13th Century. Listening Focus: Canon, Ostinato, Polyphonic Texture
Free Resources for Listening Activities & Watching Videos
* Workbook Pages - Life and Music of Josquin des Prez; "El grillo" by Josquin des Prez. Listening Focus: Frottola, Word Painting
Free Resources for Listening Activities & Watching Videos
* Workbook Pages - "Kaboran (Gamelan Prawa)" - the Javanese Gamelan. Listening Focus: Gamelan, Metallophones
Free Resources for Listening Activities & Watching Videos
* Workbook Pages - "Evening Raga: Bhopali" - the Raga in Indian music. Listening Focus: Raga, Tala, Sitar
Free Resources for Listening Activities & Watching Videos
* Workbook Pages - Music Eras Overview - Style & Characteristics
* Bonus Game - Music History Composition/Composer Review

Review Tests & Final Exam
- 12 Accumulative Review Tests (1 with each of the 12 Lessons)
* UMT Level 8 Theory Exam
* UMT Exam Series - Advanced Rudiments

Go to: UltimateMusicTheory.com FREE RESOURCES for all UMT Supplemental Workbook LEVELS for Listening Activities & Watching Videos to help you with completing all Music History/Appreciation studies.

Get your UltimateMusicTheoryApp.com - Over 7000 Flashcards including audio! Learn Faster with all 6 Subjects: Beginner - Prep, Basic, Intermediate, Advanced, Ear Training & Music Trivia (including History).

ROOT/QUALITY and FUNCTIONAL CHORD SYMBOLS (Use after Advanced Rudiments Page 59)

Review Pages 28 to 39 of the **Ultimate Music Theory LEVEL 7 Supplemental Workbook**: Chords.

Root/Quality Chord Symbols and **Functional Chord Symbols** have two different functions.

Root/Quality Chord Symbols use letters (and symbols) to indicate the Root, chord note names, Bass Note and Type/Quality.

When no Major or minor Key (Key Signature) has been established, only the Root/Quality Chord Symbol of a chord can be identified.

A Root/Quality Chord Symbol without an established Key Signature can be found in any key containing the same note names.

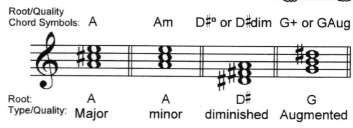

Functional Chord Symbols use Roman Numerals (and symbols) of the Scale Degree on which a chord is built to indicate the Root, Type/Quality and Position of the chord.

When the Major or minor Key (Key Signature) has been established, the Root/Quality and Functional Chord Symbols can be identified.

A chord with an established Key Signature will belong to either the Major or minor Key.

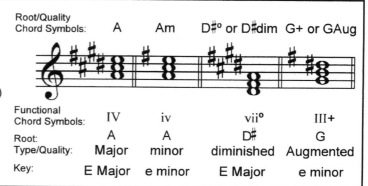

So-La Says: A Chord (Triad) can be written in **root position** or in an **inversion**.

In a Root/Quality Chord Symbol, a **Slash Chord** indicates an inversion (that a note other than the Root note is the lowest note of the chord). The letter name after the slash (" / ") is the name of the lowest note of the chord.

In Functional Chord Symbols, inversions are indicated using **Figured Bass Numbers**.

Root Position: no number; First Inversion: ^{6}; Second Inversion: $^6_4$.

1. The following triads are written without establishing a Major or minor Key Signature. For each triad:
    a) Identify the Root, Type/Quality (Maj, min, Aug or dim) and Position (root pos, 1ˢᵗ inv or 2ⁿᵈ inv).
    b) Write the Root/Quality Chord Symbol above each triad.

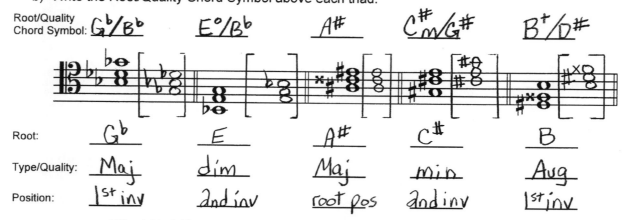

FUNCTIONAL CHORD SYMBOLS & ROOT/QUALITY CHORD SYMBOLS REVIEW - SCALES
(Use after Advanced Rudiments Page 59)

At this level, triads will be built on the Major, natural minor and harmonic minor scales only.

Scale Degree Numbers	Major Scale Functional Chord Symbol	Harmonic Minor Scale Functional Chord Symbol	Natural Minor Scale Functional Chord Symbol
$\hat{8}$	(Upper) Tonic VIII (I) = Major	(Upper) Tonic viii (i) = minor	(Upper) Tonic viii (i) = minor
$\hat{7}$	Leading Tone vii° = diminished	Leading Tone vii° = diminished	Subtonic VII = Major
$\hat{6}$	Submediant vi = minor	Submediant VI = Major	Submediant VI = Major
$\hat{5}$	Dominant V = Major	Dominant V = Major	Dominant v = minor
$\hat{4}$	Subdominant IV = Major	Subdominant iv = minor	Subdominant iv = minor
$\hat{3}$	Mediant iii = minor	Mediant III+ = Augmented	Mediant III = Major
$\hat{2}$	Supertonic ii = minor	Supertonic ii° = diminished	Supertonic ii° = diminished
$\hat{1}$	(Lower) Tonic I = Major	(Lower) Tonic i = minor	(Lower) Tonic i = minor

1. Write the Root/Quality Chord Symbol above each triad and the Functional Chord Symbol below.

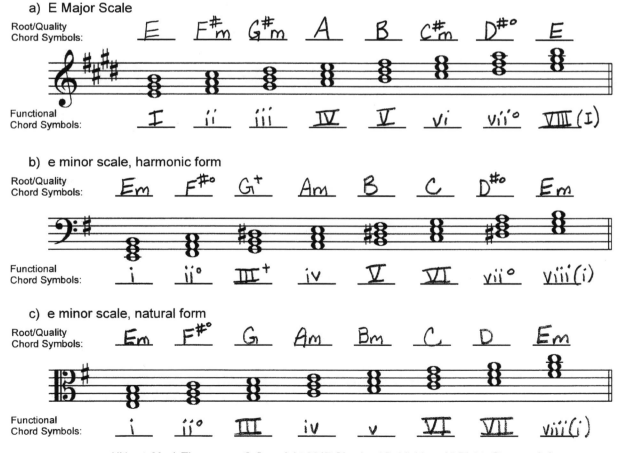

a) E Major Scale

Root/Quality Chord Symbols: E   F#m   G#m   A   B   C#m   D#°   E

Functional Chord Symbols: I   ii   iii   IV   V   vi   vii°   VIII(I)

b) e minor scale, harmonic form

Root/Quality Chord Symbols: Em   F#°   G+   Am   B   C   D#°   Em

Functional Chord Symbols: i   ii°   III+   iv   V   VI   vii°   viii(i)

c) e minor scale, natural form

Root/Quality Chord Symbols: Em   F#°   G   Am   Bm   C   D   Em

Functional Chord Symbols: i   ii°   III   iv   v   VI   VII   viii(i)

TRIADS and HARMONIC MINOR SCALES (Use after Advanced Rudiments page 59)

An accidental affects the note on that line or in that space until it is canceled by a bar line or by another accidental. When writing the **triads** of the **harmonic minor scale**, it is necessary to write the accidental for the **raised Leading Tone** on each of the 3 triads (III+, V and vii°).

When a natural sign is used on the root note of the triad, it is not required when writing the Root/Quality Chord Symbol letter name above the triad. (All other accidentals are required.)

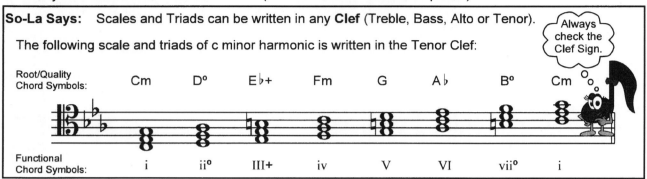

So-La Says: Scales and Triads can be written in any **Clef** (Treble, Bass, Alto or Tenor).

The following scale and triads of c minor harmonic is written in the Tenor Clef:

1. a) Write the following scales ascending one octave. Use a Key Signature and any necessary accidentals. Use whole notes. Write a root position triad above each scale degree note.
   b) Write the Root/Quality Chord Symbol above and the Functional Chord Symbol below each triad.

   i) g♯ minor scale, harmonic form, in the Alto Clef.

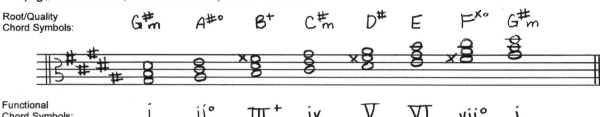

   ii) d♯ minor scale, harmonic form, in the Tenor Clef.

   iii) a♭ minor scale, harmonic form, in the Bass Clef.

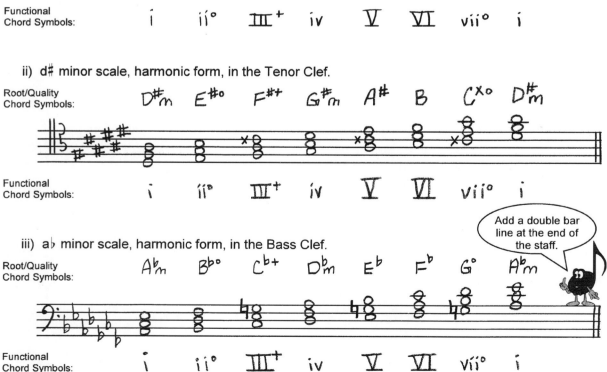

TRIAD QUALITY and SCALE DEGREE QUIZ (Use after Advanced Rudiments page 59)

♫ **Ti-Do Tip:** The following Chart shows where the Triad Type/Qualities are found in each type of scale:

Triad Type/Qualities:	Major scale	minor scale, harmonic form	minor scale, natural form
Major Triad:	I, IV, V	V, VI	III, VI, VII
Minor Triad:	ii, iii, vi	i, iv	i, iv, v
Augmented Triad:		III+	
Diminished Triad:	vii°	ii°, vii°	ii°

1. For each Triad, write the Triad Type/Quality, Functional Chord Symbol and Root/Quality Chord Symbol.

	Triad	Type/Quality	Functional Chord Symbol	Root/Quality Chord Symbol
EX:	Submediant Triad of C♭ Major:	minor	vi	A♭m
a)	Supertonic Triad of D Major:	minor	ii	Em
b)	Subtonic Triad of d minor, natural form:	Major	VII	C
c)	Leading Tone Triad of d minor, harmonic form:	diminished	vii°	C#°
d)	Submediant Triad of d minor, natural form:	Major	VI	B♭
e)	Submediant Triad of d minor, harmonic form:	Major	VI	B♭
f)	Tonic Triad of B Major:	Major	I	B
g)	Tonic Triad of b minor, harmonic form:	minor	i	Bm
h)	Tonic Triad of b minor, natural form:	minor	i	Bm
i)	Mediant Triad of a minor, natural form:	Major	III	C
j)	Mediant Triad of a minor, harmonic form:	Augmented	III+	C+
k)	Mediant Triad of A Major:	minor	iii	C#m
l)	Subdominant Triad of e♭ minor, harmonic form:	minor	iv	A♭m
m)	Subdominant Triad of e♭ minor, natural form:	minor	iv	A♭m
n)	Subdominant Triad of E Major:	Major	IV	A
o)	Dominant Triad of b♭ minor, natural form:	minor	v	Fm
p)	Dominant Triad of b minor, harmonic form:	Major	V	F#
q)	Dominant Triad of B♭ Major:	Major	V	F
r)	Supertonic Triad of a# minor, harmonic form:	diminished	ii°	B#°
s)	Supertonic Triad of a♭ minor, natural form:	diminished	ii°	B♭°
t)	Leading Tone Triad of F# Major:	diminished	vii°	E#°

FUNCTIONAL CHORD SYMBOLS & ROOT/QUALITY CHORD SYMBOLS REVIEW - TRIADS
(Use after Advanced Rudiments Page 59)

Triads can be written using a Key Signature. An accidental will be required for the raised Leading Tone (Leading Note) in a minor (harmonic) key.

A **Key Signature** is written at the beginning of the music. When an exercise has a Key Signature change for every measure, a different Key Signature will be used at the beginning of each measure.

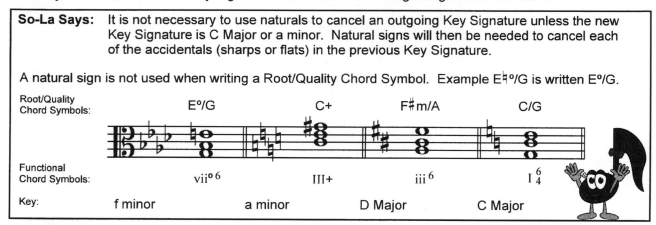

> **So-La Says:** It is not necessary to use naturals to cancel an outgoing Key Signature unless the new Key Signature is C Major or a minor. Natural signs will then be needed to cancel each of the accidentals (sharps or flats) in the previous Key Signature.
>
> A natural sign is not used when writing a Root/Quality Chord Symbol. Example E♮°/G is written E°/G.

1. a) Write the Key Signature for each measure.
   b) Observing the Functional Chord Symbol, write each triad. Use whole notes.
   c) Write the Root/Quality Chord Symbol above each triad.

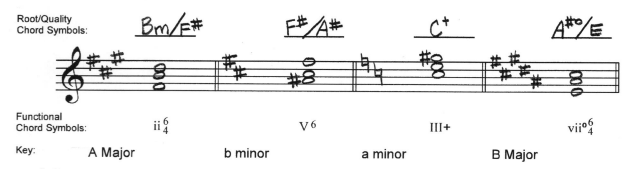

♫ **Ti-Do Tip:** In the **natural form** of a minor scale, the 7th scale degree (the Subtonic) is not raised.

2. Write the following triads in root position. Use Key Signatures and any necessary accidentals. Use whole notes. Write the Root/Quality Chord Symbol above and the Functional Chord Symbol below.

   a) the Leading Tone triad of g minor, harmonic form
   b) the Mediant triad of d minor, natural form
   c) the Supertonic triad of C Major
   d) the Subtonic triad of c minor, natural form

> Be careful. Is it:
> Major? Minor Natural?
> or Minor Harmonic?

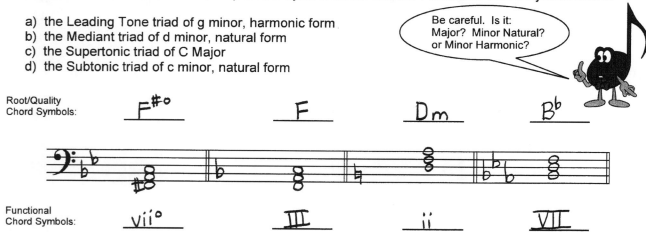

FUNCTIONAL CHORD SYMBOLS & ROOT/QUALITY CHORD SYMBOLS - KEYBOARD STYLE
(Use after Advanced Rudiments Page 59)

A chord written in **Keyboard Style** has one note in the Bass Staff and three notes in the Treble Staff. The position of the chord is always based upon the note written in the Bass (the lowest note of the chord).

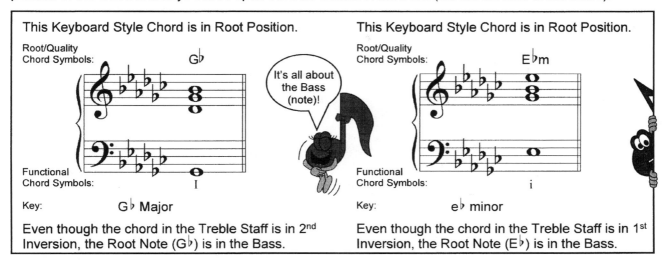

The Standard Interval Distance (the preferred distance) between the Bass Note and the lowest note of the chord in the Treble Staff is no larger than an interval of a 12th. It is acceptable to have a larger interval distance (an interval of a 13th to 15th). The interval should not be greater than 2 octaves.

1. For each of the following Keyboard Style Tonic, Subdominant and Dominant Chords:
   a) Name the Major or minor key.
   b) Write the Root/Quality Chord Symbol above the staff and the Functional Chord Symbol below.

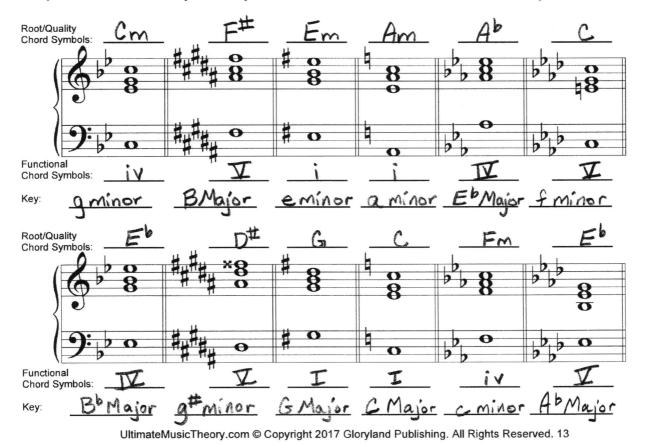

OPEN and CLOSE POSITION CHORD REVIEW (Use after Advanced Rudiments page 59)

Review Pages 40 and 41 of the **Ultimate Music Theory LEVEL 7 Supplemental Workbook**: Open to Close Position Chords.

Chords can be written in either **Close Position** (as close together as possible) or in **Open Position** (spread out within a single staff or on the Grand Staff).

One form of Open Position is called Chorale Style or SATB Style. In Chorale Style, each of the notes of the chord represents a singing voice: Soprano, Alto, Tenor and Bass.

The Soprano and Alto notes (voices or parts) are written in the Treble Staff. The Tenor and Bass notes (voices or parts) are written in the Bass Staff.

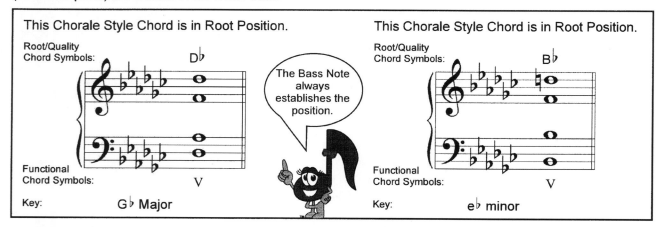

The notes in the Soprano, Alto and Tenor voices can be in any order. There will be more than one correct answer for the placement of the Soprano, Alto and Tenor notes when writing a Chord in Chorale Style.

The Standard Interval Distances (the preferred distances) between the notes (voices or parts) is:
Soprano and Alto = Perfect 1 to Perfect 8;
Alto and Tenor = Perfect 1 to Perfect 8;
Tenor and Bass = Perfect 1 to Perfect 12.

1. For each of the following Keyboard Style Tonic, Subdominant and Dominant Chords:
   a) Name the Major or minor key.
   b) Write the Root/Quality Chord Symbol above the staff and the Functional Chord Symbol below.

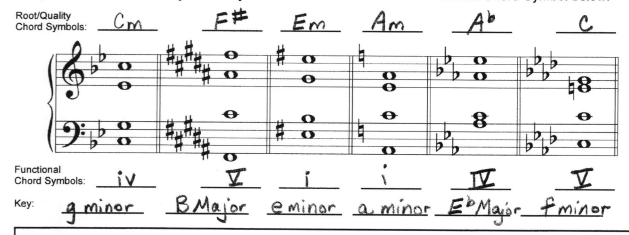

♫ **Ti-Do Time:** Your Teacher will play the chords on Pages 13 & 14. Listen to the Keyboard and Chorale Style Chords. Identify the quality as Major or minor.

STEMS - KEYBOARD and CHORALE STYLE CHORDS (Use after Advanced Rudiments page 59)

A 4-note Chord written in **Keyboard Style** will use stems that follow the Stem Rule. The stem direction for the chord in the Treble Staff is based upon the note that is the furthest away from the middle line.

When the note furthest away from the middle line is below the middle line, the stem for the chord goes up.
When the note furthest away from the middle line is above the middle line, the stem for the chord goes down.

♫ **Ti-Do Tip:**   For a 4-note Chord written in **Chorale Style**:

   Stems will go up for the Soprano and Tenor notes (voices or parts);
   Stems will go down for the Alto and Bass notes (voices or parts).

The purpose of these stems is to allow singers to easily follow their notes (voices or parts) when singing.

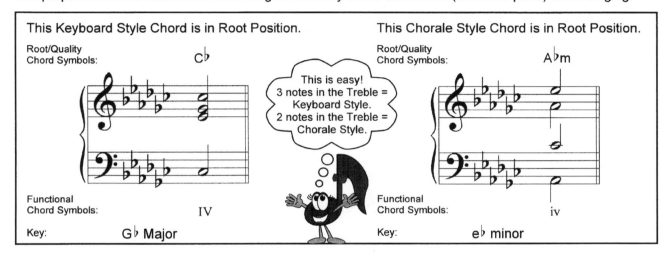

1. For each of the following Keyboard or Chorale Style Tonic, Subdominant and Dominant Chords:
   a) Circle if the chord is in Keyboard or Chorale Style.
   b) Add stems to create half notes.
   c) Name the Major or minor key.
   d) Write the Root/Quality Chord Symbol above the staff and the Functional Chord Symbol below.

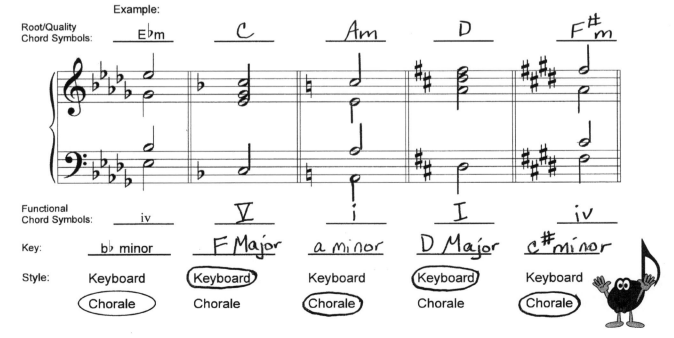

DOTS - KEYBOARD and CHORALE STYLE CHORDS (Use after Advanced Rudiments page 59)

For notes in **Keyboard Style**, dots to form dotted half notes (or dotted quarter notes) follow the Standard Dot Placement Rules. Dots are written to the right of each notehead, in the space above the note for a line note and in the same space for a space note.

The Dot Placement Rules for notes in **Chorale (SATB) Style** are different.

For the Soprano and Tenor notes (voices or parts), dots are written to the right of each notehead, in the space above the note for a line note and in the same space for a space note.

For the Alto and Bass notes (voices or parts), dots are written to the right of each notehead in the space **below** the note for a line note and in the same space for a space note.

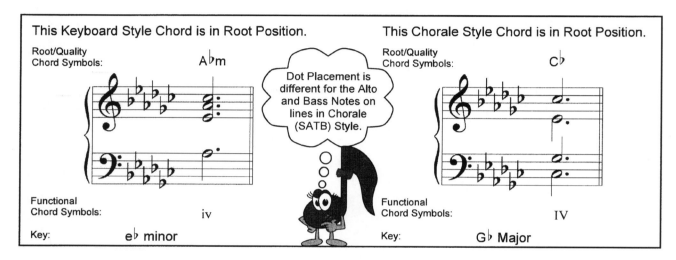

1. For each of the following Keyboard or Chorale Style Tonic, Subdominant and Dominant Chords:
   a) Circle if the chord is in Keyboard or Chorale Style.
   b) Add stems and dots to create dotted half notes.
   c) Name the Major or minor key.
   d) Write the Root/Quality Chord Symbol above the staff and the Functional Chord Symbol below.

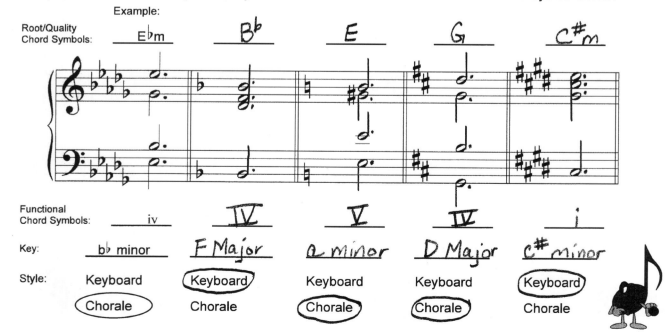

WRITING KEYBOARD and CHORALE STYLE CHORDS (Use after Advanced Rudiments page 59)

When writing a Chord in Keyboard or Chorale (SATB) Style, **4 notes** are used. The root note of the chord is written in the Bass (for Root Position Chords). When converting a triad to a 4-note chord, the most common note to double (write twice) is the root note (although the third or fifth note can sometimes be doubled).

The Leading Tone (Leading Note, or scale degree $\hat{7}$) is never doubled (repeated or written twice).

1. Write each chord in Root Position in Chorale (SATB) Style. Use a Key Signature and any necessary accidentals. Use dotted half notes. There will be more than one correct answer for each chord.
(one possible answer for each below)

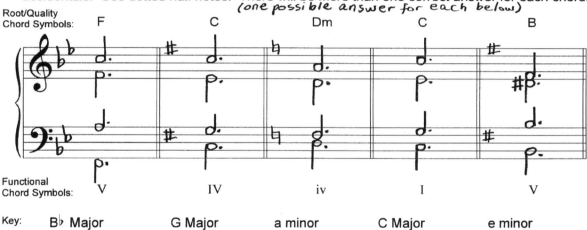

2. For each of the following minor keys, write the chord in Keyboard Style. Use dotted half notes. Use accidentals if necessary. There will be more than one correct answer for each chord.
(one possible answer for each below)

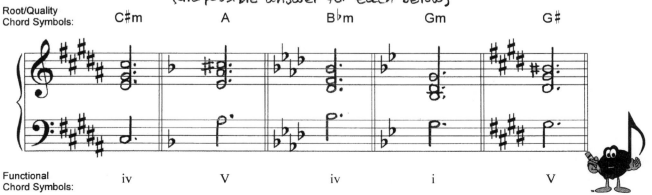

FUNCTIONAL CHORD SYMBOLS - DOMINANT 7th & LEADING-TONE DIMINISHED 7th CHORDS
(Use after Advanced Rudiments Page 69)

A 7th Chord is a 4-note chord that is built using 4 different note names - a root, third, fifth and seventh. The term "7th Chord" comes from that distance (interval) of a 7th.

At this level, there are 2 types (or qualities) of 7th Chords - the Dominant 7th Chord and the Leading-Tone Diminished 7th Chord.

The **Dominant 7th Chord** is built on the Dominant note (scale degree $\hat{5}$) of the Major and of the harmonic minor scales. In the minor key, this chord will contain the raised Leading Tone (scale degree $\hat{7}$).

The **Leading-Tone Diminished 7th Chord** (or the Diminished 7th Chord) is built on the raised Leading Tone (the Leading Note, scale degree $\hat{7}$) of the harmonic minor scale.

♫ **Ti-Do Tip:**   At this level, the Dominant 7th Chord will be written and identified in Root Position, First Inversion, Second Inversion and Third Inversion. The Leading-Tone Diminished 7th Chord will be written and identified only in Root Position.

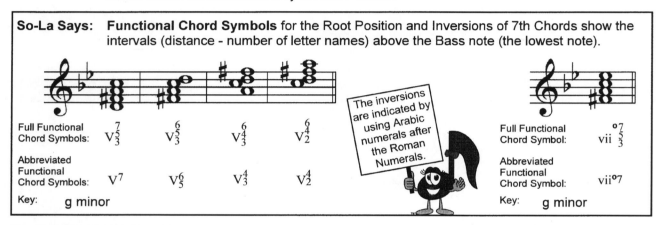

So-La Says: **Functional Chord Symbols** for the Root Position and Inversions of 7th Chords show the intervals (distance - number of letter names) above the Bass note (the lowest note).

The Full Functional Chord Symbols show the intervals above the Bass note. It is preferred to use the **Abbreviated Functional Chord Symbols** when identifying the positions of the 7th Chords.

1. For each of the following 7th Chords:
   a) Name the Major or minor key.
   b) Write the Functional Chord Symbol below. (Use the Abbreviated Functional Chord Symbols.)

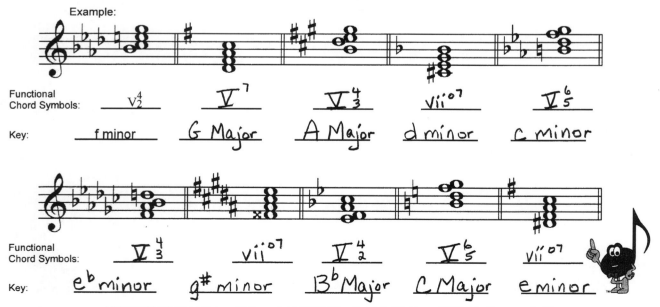

FUNCTIONAL CHORD SYMBOLS & ROOT/QUALITY CHORD SYMBOLS - 7th CHORDS
(Use after Advanced Rudiments Page 69)

When writing the **Root/Quality Chord Symbol** for a **Dominant 7th Chord**, an Upper Case letter followed by a "7" is used for a Root Position Chord. A Slash Chord is used for an inversion. The letter name after the slash (" / ") is the name of the note written at the bottom (the lowest note) of the 7th Chord inversion.

When writing the **Root/Quality Chord Symbol** for a **Leading-Tone Diminished 7th Chord**, an Upper Case letter followed by a "°7" is used. At this level, the Leading-Tone Diminished 7th Chord is written only in Root Position and is written only in the minor key (using the notes of the harmonic minor scale).

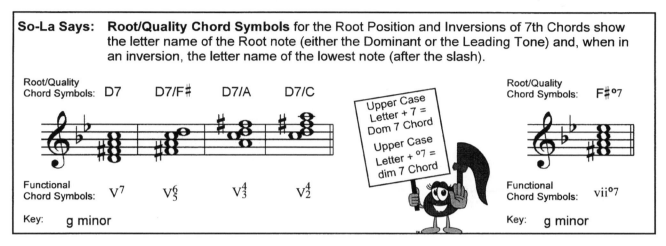

So-La Says: **Root/Quality Chord Symbols** for the Root Position and Inversions of 7th Chords show the letter name of the Root note (either the Dominant or the Leading Tone) and, when in an inversion, the letter name of the lowest note (after the slash).

A Dominant 7th Chord or a Leading-Tone Diminished 7th Chord written in **Close Position** is written on one staff, with notes written as close together as possible. Harmonic Intervals (distances) will be a 2nd or a 3rd.

1. For each of the following 7th Chords:
   a) Name the Major or minor key.
   b) Write the Root/Quality Chord Symbol above the staff and the Functional Chord Symbol below.

NOTE PLACEMENT for 7th CHORDS and INVERSIONS (Use after Advanced Rudiments Page 69)

Review Pages 34 and 35 of the **Ultimate Music Theory LEVEL 7 Supplemental Workbook**: Note Placement and Accidental Placement for Dominant Seventh Chords and Inversions.

Dominant 7th Chords and Leading-Tone Diminished 7th Chords can be written using a Key Signature (and any necessary accidentals for the raised Leading Tone in a minor key) or written using only accidentals.

Dominant 7th Chords and Leading-Tone Diminished 7th Chords can be written using note values other than a whole note.

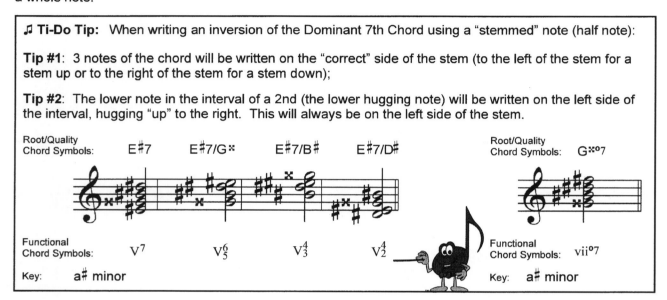

♫ **Ti-Do Tip:** When writing an inversion of the Dominant 7th Chord using a "stemmed" note (half note):

Tip #1: 3 notes of the chord will be written on the "correct" side of the stem (to the left of the stem for a stem up or to the right of the stem for a stem down);

Tip #2: The lower note in the interval of a 2nd (the lower hugging note) will be written on the left side of the interval, hugging "up" to the right. This will always be on the left side of the stem.

In **Close Position**, the stem is written in the direction of the note that is furthest away from the middle line. By adding a stem, it is easy to see if the note placement for a 7th Chord Inversion is correct or incorrect.

1. For each Dominant 7th Chord inversion, circle if the note placement is Correct or Incorrect.

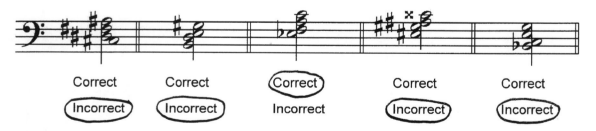

2. Write the following 7th Chords. Use half notes. Use accidentals.

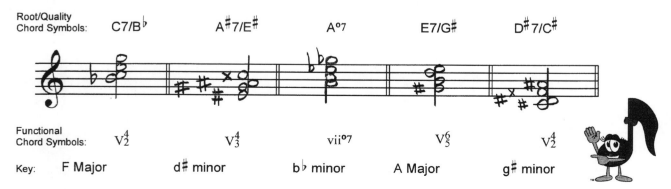

DOT PLACEMENT for 7th CHORD INVERSIONS (Use after Advanced Rudiments Page 69)

When writing 7th Chords in Close Position using dotted note values (like a dotted quarter note or a dotted half note), each of the notes will have its own dot.

Standard Dot Placement Rules: Dots are written to the right of each notehead, in the space above the note for a line note and in the same space for a space note.

In a **7th Chord Inversion**, when the lowest note is written on a **line**, dots are written to the right of each notehead, in the space **below** the note for a line note and in the same space for a space note.

In a **7th Chord Inversion**, when the lowest note is written in a **space**, all dots will follow the Standard Dot Placement Rules.

Lowest note is on a line = the dots for the line notes will be written in the space below the line.	Lowest note is in a space = the dots for the line notes will be written in the space above the line.

When written using a **Key Signature**, a Dominant 7th Chord belongs to either the Major or relative minor key. When written using **accidentals**, a Dominant 7th Chord belongs to both the Major and Tonic (parallel) minor keys. A Leading-Tone Diminished 7th Chord is found in a Harmonic minor scale. In a minor key with a **Key Signature**, the Leading Tone (7th) will be raised a chromatic half step using an **accidental**.

1. For each of the following Dominant 7th Chord inversions (written using accidentals):
   a) Add stems and dots to create dotted half notes.
   b) Name the Major and the minor key.
   c) Write the Root/Quality Chord Symbol above the staff and the Functional Chord Symbol below.

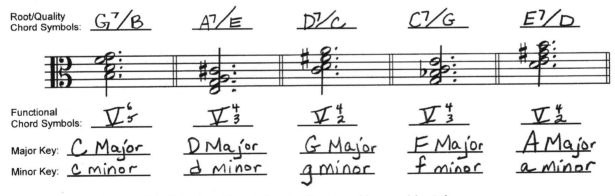

2. Write the following 7th Chords. Use dotted half notes. Use accidentals.

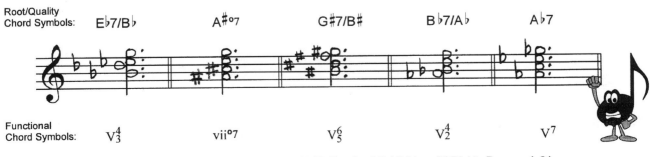

COMPLETE and INCOMPLETE 7th CHORDS (Use after Advanced Rudiments Page 69)

A Dominant 7th Chord in Keyboard or Chorale Style can be written in Complete Form or in Incomplete Form.

Complete Form of a Dominant 7th Chord = Root ($\hat{5}$), Third ($\hat{7}$), Fifth ($\hat{2}$) and Seventh ($\hat{4}$).

Incomplete Form of a Dominant 7th Chord = Root ($\hat{5}$), Root ($\hat{5}$), Third ($\hat{7}$) and Seventh ($\hat{4}$). The Root (scale degree $\hat{5}$) is doubled and the Fifth (scale degree $\hat{2}$) is omitted.

A **Leading-Tone Diminished 7th Chord** (built using the notes of the harmonic minor scale) is written in **Complete Form** = Root ($\hat{7}$), Third ($\hat{2}$), Fifth ($\hat{4}$) and Seventh ($\hat{6}$). The Root (scale degree $\hat{7}$) is raised.

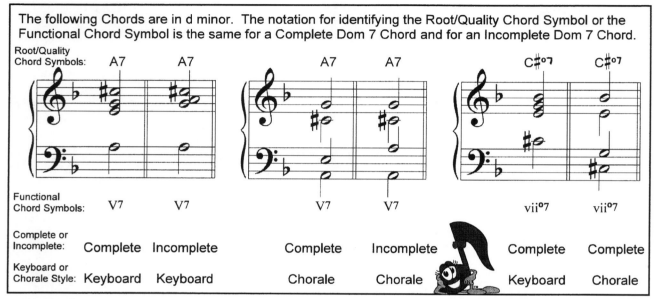

1. For each of the following 7th Chords:
   a) Name the Major or minor key.
   b) Name the Root. The Root will be either the Dominant ($\hat{5}$) or the Leading Tone ($\hat{7}$) of the Key.
   c) Name the Quality/Type of Chord as Dominant 7th (Dom 7) or as Leading-Tone Diminished 7th (dim 7).
   d) Name the Form as Complete or Incomplete.
   e) Name the Style as Keyboard or Chorale.

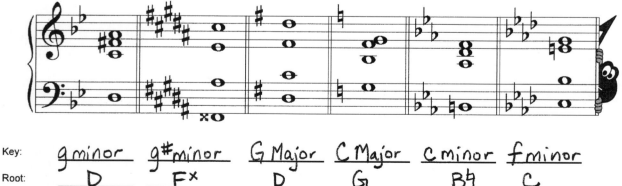

Key:	g minor	g# minor	G Major	C Major	C minor	f minor
Root:	D	Fx	D	G	B♮	C
Quality/Type:	Dom 7	dim 7	Dom 7	Dom 7	dim 7	Dom 7
Complete or Incomplete:	Complete	Complete	Incomplete	Incomplete	Complete	Complete
Keyboard or Chorale:	Keyboard	Chorale	Chorale	Keyboard	Keyboard	Chorale

CHORD IDENTIFICATION REVIEW (Use after Advanced Rudiments page 70)

Composers in the 20th and 21st Century expanded the Harmonic Language of Chords to include the **Quartal Chord**, the **Polychord** and the **Cluster Chord**.

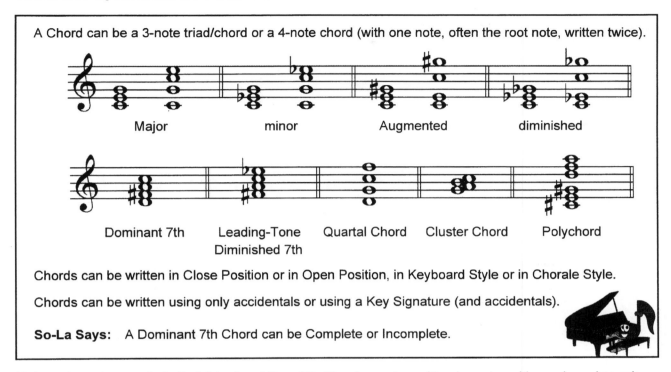

A Chord can be a 3-note triad/chord or a 4-note chord (with one note, often the root note, written twice).

Major   minor   Augmented   diminished

Dominant 7th   Leading-Tone Diminished 7th   Quartal Chord   Cluster Chord   Polychord

Chords can be written in Close Position or in Open Position, in Keyboard Style or in Chorale Style.

Chords can be written using only accidentals or using a Key Signature (and accidentals).

So-La Says: A Dominant 7th Chord can be Complete or Incomplete.

Major, minor, Augmented, diminished and Dom 7th Chords can be written in root position or in an inversion.

1. Name each of the following chords as either: Major, minor, Augmented, diminished, Dominant 7th (Dom 7), Leading-Tone diminished 7th (dim 7), Quartal Chord, Polychord or Cluster Chord.

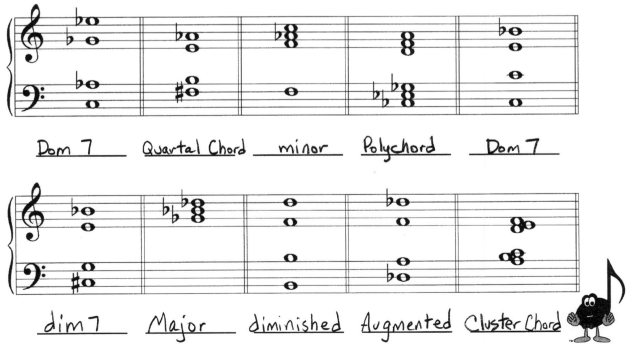

Dom 7   Quartal Chord   minor   Polychord   Dom 7

dim7   Major   diminished   Augmented   Cluster Chord

UNDERSTANDING CADENCES and THE LANGUAGE OF HARMONY
(Use after Advanced Rudiments Page 82)

Review Pages 42 to 47 of the **Ultimate Music Theory LEVEL 7 Supplemental Workbook**: Keyboard Style Authentic (Perfect) and Half (Imperfect) Cadences.

With the addition of the Language of Harmony in the Theory Syllabus, it is important that Students complete the **LEVEL 6 and LEVEL 7 Supplemental Workbooks** in order to create a foundation in Harmony.

So-La Says: A **Cadence** is a progression of two (or more) chords used at the end of a phrase.

A **Stable Scale Degree** is the Tonic ($\hat{1}$) or Mediant ($\hat{3}$) Scale Degree. **Voice Leading** refers to how voices move from one chord to another.

A **Tendency Tone** is an "active" scale degree that tends to resolve (move) by step to a less active scale degree (for example: Scale Degree $\hat{7}$ tends to resolve to Scale Degree $\hat{8}$ ($\hat{1}$) to the Tonic).

An **Authentic Cadence** (formally known as the Perfect Cadence) is a Dominant to Tonic (V - I or V - i) or Dominant 7th to Tonic (V7 - I or V7 -i) Cadence progression.

A **Half Cadence** (formally known as the Imperfect Cadence) is a Tonic to Dominant (I - V or i - V) or Subdominant to Dominant (IV - V or iv - V) Cadence progression.

A **Plagal Cadence** is a Subdominant to Tonic (IV - I or iv - i) Cadence progression.

---

1. For each of the following Keyboard Style Cadences:
   a) Write the Voice Leading Scale Degree number above each Soprano (upper/top) Cadence Voice.
   b) Write the Functional Chord Symbol below each Chord.
   c) Identify the Cadence as Authentic, Half or Plagal.

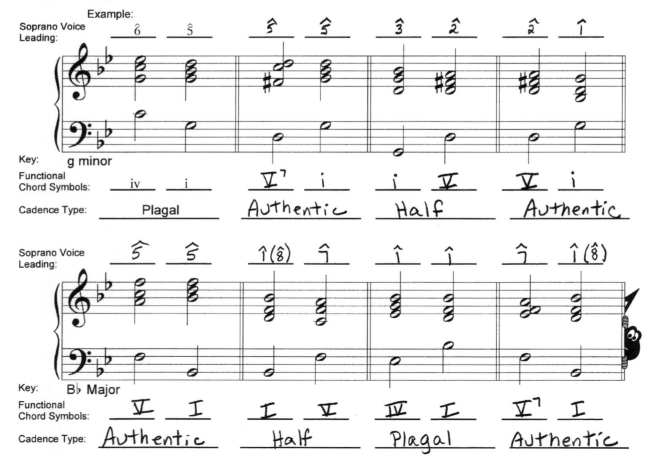

CADENCES in KEYBOARD STYLE (Use after Advanced Rudiments Page 82)

In "Harmonic Analysis", there are two types of "Authentic" Cadences – the **Perfect** Authentic Cadence (PAC) and the **Imperfect** Authentic Cadence (IAC).

In a Perfect Authentic Cadence (PAC), the Soprano Voice ends on the Tonic (Stable Scale Degree Î).

In an Imperfect Authentic Cadence (IAC), the Soprano Voice does not end on the Tonic (Scale Degree Î).

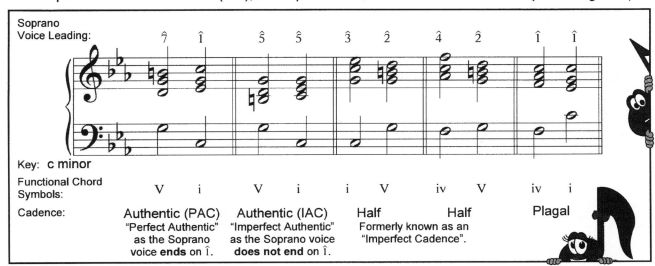

Key: c minor

Functional Chord Symbols:	V	i	V	i	i	V	iv	V	iv	i

Cadence:	Authentic (PAC)	Authentic (IAC)	Half	Half	Plagal
	"Perfect Authentic" as the Soprano voice **ends** on Î.	"Imperfect Authentic" as the Soprano voice **does not end** on Î.	Formerly known as an "Imperfect Cadence".		

1. Write the following Cadences in Keyboard Style. Use half notes (and accidentals as needed). Follow the Voice Leading Scale Degrees for the Soprano (upper/top) Cadence Voice.

Key: f♯ minor

Functional Chord Symbols:	V	i	iv	i	V	i	iv	V

Cadence Type:	Authentic (PAC)	Plagal	Authentic (IAC)	Half

Key: A Major

Functional Chord Symbols:	V	I	V	I	IV	I	I	V

Cadence Type:	Authentic (IAC)	Authentic (PAC)	Plagal	Half

CADENCE VOICE LEADING (Use after Advanced Rudiments Page 82)

"**Voice Leading**" means the gradual movement of notes between chords in a progression. Voice Leading (vocal or instrumental) is based upon the melodies of vocal music. Smooth Voice Leading between notes in the Treble Staff chords is: **Static** (same common note - *stasis*), **Conjunct** (step) or **Disjunct** (skip/leap).

The Tonic (I or i) Chord uses the Scale Degrees $\hat{1}(\hat{8})$, $\hat{3}$, $\hat{5}$.

The Subdominant (IV or iv) Chord uses the Scale Degrees $\hat{4}$, $\hat{6}$, $\hat{1}(\hat{8})$.

The Dominant (V) Chord uses the Scale Degrees $\hat{5}$, $\hat{7}$, $\hat{2}$. (Scale Degree $\hat{7}$ is raised in the minor key.)

1. Write a Keyboard Style Cadence below the bracketed melody notes. Use the correct note values. Write the Functional Chord Symbol below each chord. Name the type of Cadence (Authentic, Half or Plagal).

Static Voice Leading (movement by repetition):

Authentic Cadence (V - I , V - i): $\hat{5}\rightarrow\hat{5}$.

Half Cadence (i - V, I - V): $\hat{5}\rightarrow\hat{5}$.

Half Cadence (IV - V, iv - V): No Common Note

Plagal Cadence (IV - I, iv - i): $\hat{1}\rightarrow\hat{1}$.

Tip: Identify the Key (Major or minor). Then identify the Scale Degree Numbers (Voice Leading) in the Soprano Voice.

Conjunct Voice Leading (movement by step):

Authentic Cadence (V - I , V - i): Step down = $\hat{2}\rightarrow\hat{1}$; Step up = $\hat{7}\rightarrow\hat{8}(\hat{1})$; $\hat{2}\rightarrow\hat{3}$.

Half Cadence (i - V, I - V): Step down = $\hat{3}\rightarrow\hat{2}$; $\hat{8}(\hat{1})\rightarrow\hat{7}$; Step up = $\hat{1}\rightarrow\hat{2}$.

Half Cadence (IV - V, iv - V): Step down = $\hat{6}\rightarrow\hat{5}$; $\hat{8}(\hat{1})\rightarrow\hat{7}$.

Plagal Cadence (IV - I, iv - i): Step down = $\hat{6}\rightarrow\hat{5}$; $\hat{4}\rightarrow\hat{3}$.

Tip: Contrary Motion movement between the Treble and Bass Voices is best.

Disjunct Voice Leading (movement by skip):

Authentic Cadence (V - I , V - i): Skip down = $\hat{5}\searrow\hat{3}$.
(*Preferable to not use $\hat{7}\searrow\hat{5}$ as the final melody line.)

Half Cadence (i - V, I - V): Skip up = $\hat{3}\nearrow\hat{5}$; $\hat{5}\nearrow\hat{7}$.

Half Cadence (IV - V, iv - V): Skip down = $\hat{4}\searrow\hat{2}$.

Plagal Cadence (IV - I, iv - i): No Disjunct movement.

---

a) In the key of f# minor:

Functional Chord Symbols: iv   i

Cadence Type: Plagal

b) In the key of A♭ Major:

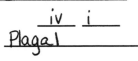

Functional Chord Symbols: I   V

Cadence Type: Half

c) In the key of b minor:

Functional Chord Symbols: V   i

Cadence Type: Authentic

CHORALE STYLE CADENCES (Use after Advanced Rudiments Page 82)

Review Page 40 of the **Ultimate Music Theory LEVEL 7 Supplemental Workbook**: Open Position Chords.

A Cadence can be written in Keyboard Style or in Chorale Style.

Keyboard Style Chord: One note in the Bass Staff (the Root) and a 3-note Triad in the Treble Staff. The 3-note triad is written in Close Position - notes are as close together as possible (up to an octave).

Chorale Style Chord (or SATB): 2 notes in the Treble Staff (Soprano Voice - Stem Up; Alto Voice - Stem Down) and 2 notes in the Bass Staff (Tenor Voice - Stem Up; Bass Voice - Stem Down). When both voices in the same staff have the same note, two stems (Stem Up and Stem Down) are used for one single note.

Chorale Style Chord written in Open Position - notes are "spread out", with intervals of a 5th or larger between two neighboring voices. When written in Close Position - SAT notes are written within one octave.

So-La Says: Chorale Style is written for 4 "singing" voices. Notes for each SATB (Soprano, Alto, Tenor, Bass) voice should be kept within the **Standard Singing (Vocal) Range** for that voice:

Soprano: **Alto:** **Tenor:** **Bass:**

♫ **Ti-Do Tip:** The notes in each SATB Chord in a Chorale Style Cadence should observe the **Standard Interval Distances** between the voices:

Soprano and Alto Voices = Perfect 1 to Perfect 8;

Alto to Tenor Voices = Perfect 1 to Perfect 8;

Tenor to Bass Voices = Perfect 1 to Perfect 12.

The best Voice Leading between notes in the Soprano, Alto and Tenor voices, with a change of harmony, is smoothly: **Static** (same), **Conjunct** (step) or **Disjunct** (skip/leap). The best Voice Leading between notes in the Bass voices is to move in **Contrary Motion** to the Soprano, Alto and/or Tenor Voices.

1. For each of the following Chorale Style Cadences:
    a) Write the Voice Leading Scale Degree number above each Soprano (upper/top) Cadence Voice.
    b) Write the Functional Chord Symbol below each Chord.
    c) Identify the Cadence as Authentic, Half or Plagal.

CROSSED VOICE PROGRESSION ERRORS (Use after Advanced Rudiments Page 82)

When writing Cadences in Chorale Style, the pitch or vocal range for each of the four Voice Progressions (Soprano, Alto, Tenor and Bass) cannot "**Cross Voices**".

The Soprano Voice (stems up in the Treble) is the highest voice (the highest pitched voice progression);

The Alto Voice (stems down in the Treble) is pitched lower than the Soprano and higher than the Tenor;

The Tenor Voice (stems up in the Bass) is pitched lower than the Alto and higher than the Bass;

The Bass Voice (stems down in the Bass) is the lowest voice (the lowest pitched voice progression).

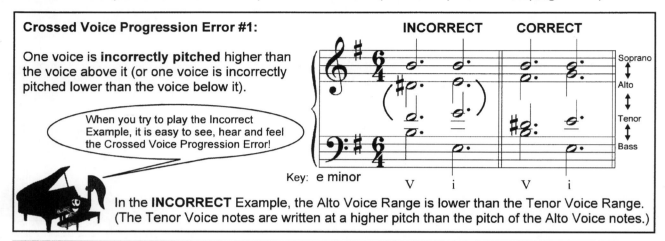

Crossed Voice Progression Error #1:

One voice is **incorrectly pitched** higher than the voice above it (or one voice is incorrectly pitched lower than the voice below it).

When you try to play the Incorrect Example, it is easy to see, hear and feel the Crossed Voice Progression Error!

In the **INCORRECT** Example, the Alto Voice Range is lower than the Tenor Voice Range. (The Tenor Voice notes are written at a higher pitch than the pitch of the Alto Voice notes.)

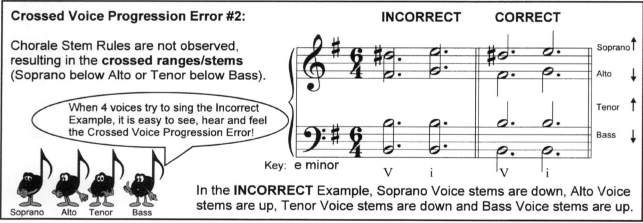

Crossed Voice Progression Error #2:

Chorale Stem Rules are not observed, resulting in the **crossed ranges/stems** (Soprano below Alto or Tenor below Bass).

When 4 voices try to sing the Incorrect Example, it is easy to see, hear and feel the Crossed Voice Progression Error!

In the **INCORRECT** Example, Soprano Voice stems are down, Alto Voice stems are up, Tenor Voice stems are down and Bass Voice stems are up.

1. Indicate whether the Voice Progressions in each Authentic Cadence in d minor are Correct or Incorrect.

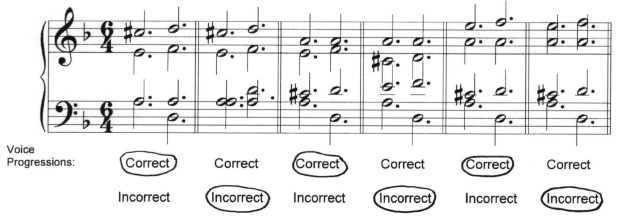

Voice Progressions:

(Correct)   Correct   (Correct)   Correct   (Correct)   Correct

Incorrect   (Incorrect)   Incorrect   (Incorrect)   Incorrect   (Incorrect)

WRITING CADENCES in CHORALE STYLE (Use after Advanced Rudiments Page 82)

The Dot Placement Rules for notes in **Chorale Style** applies to each Chord in a Chorale Style Cadence.

> **So-La Says:** For the Soprano and Tenor notes (voices or parts), dots are written to the right of each notehead, in the space above the note for a line note and in the same space for a space note.
>
> For the Alto and Bass notes (voices or parts), dots are written to the right of each notehead in the space **below** the note for a line note and in the same space for a space note.

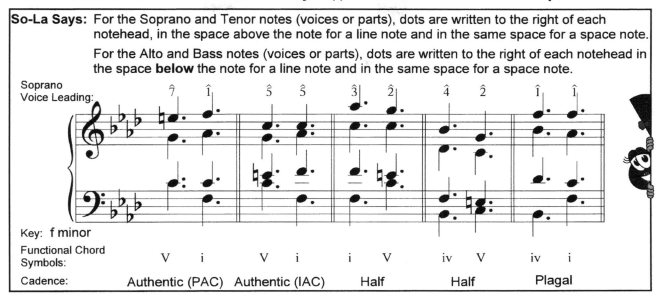

1. Write the following Cadences in Chorale Style. Use dotted quarter notes (and accidentals as needed). Follow the Voice Leading Scale Degrees for the Soprano (upper/top) Cadence Voice. There will be more than one correct answer. *(one possible answer for each below)*

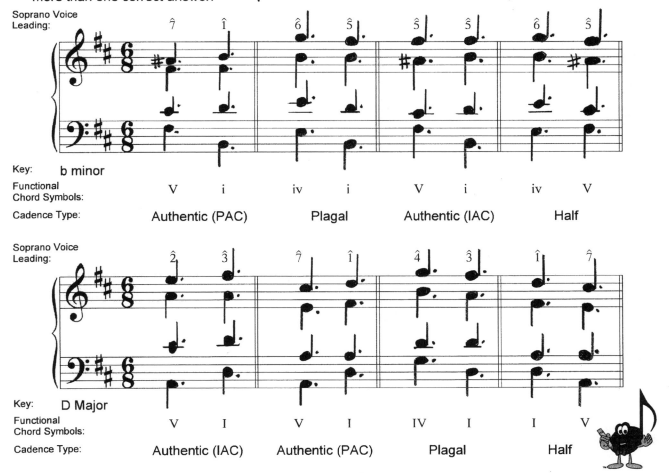

DOMINANT SEVENTH to TONIC CADENCES (Use after Advanced Rudiments Page 82)

An Authentic Cadence progression from the Dominant 7th to Tonic is a strong "final" ending for a melody.

The Dominant 7 Chord contains 2 Tendency Tones. A **Tendency Tone** is an "active" scale degree that tends to resolve (move) by step to a less active scale degree (usually to notes of the Tonic Triad).

Tendency Tone #1: The Leading Tone, Scale Degree $\hat{7}$, is the "3rd of V7" Chord.

Tendency Tone #2: The Subdominant, Scale Degree $\hat{4}$, is the "7th of V7" Chord.

♫ **Ti-Do Tip:** Bass is always Dominant to Tonic in V7 - I/i Chord.

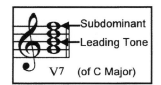

In order to correctly resolve the Tendency Tones when writing a Cadence:

An **Incomplete** Dominant Seventh Chord ($\hat{5}$, $\hat{5}$, $\hat{7}$, $\hat{4}$) will resolve to a **Complete** Tonic Chord ($\hat{1}$, $\hat{1}$, $\hat{3}$, $\hat{5}$); or

A **Complete** Dominant Seventh Chord ($\hat{5}$, $\hat{7}$, $\hat{2}$, $\hat{4}$) will resolve to an **Incomplete** Tonic Chord ($\hat{1}$, $\hat{1}$, $\hat{1}$, $\hat{3}$).

In an Authentic Cadence, the voices in the V7 to I/i chord in the Treble Staff can be written in different positions (order of notes) as long as the **Tendency Tone Rules** are observed.
(Review Page 45 in the **Ultimate Music Theory LEVEL 7 Supplemental Workbook**.)

Cadence	Chord Progression	Triad Scale Degrees	Authentic Cadence Voice Leading
Authentic Cadence	Major: V7 - I Minor: V7 - i	V7 (Incomplete Dominant Seventh): $\hat{5}$, $\hat{7}$, $\hat{4}$ ($\hat{5}$ in Bass, omit the $\hat{2}$) to I/i (Complete Tonic): $\hat{1}$, $\hat{3}$, $\hat{5}$ ($\hat{1}$ in Bass)	$\hat{4} \searrow \hat{3}$ $\hat{7} \nearrow \hat{1}$ $\hat{5} \to \hat{5}$ Bass to ascend OR Bass to descend $\hat{5} \nearrow \hat{1}$ $\hat{5} \searrow \hat{1}$
Authentic Cadence	Major: V7 - I Minor: V7 - i	V7 (Complete Dominant Seventh): $\hat{5}$, $\hat{7}$, $\hat{2}$, $\hat{4}$ to I/i (Incomplete Tonic): $\hat{1}$, $\hat{1}$, $\hat{3}$ ($\hat{1}$ in Bass, omit the $\hat{5}$)	$\hat{4} \searrow \hat{3}$ $\hat{2} \searrow \hat{1}$ $\hat{7} \nearrow \hat{1}$ Bass to ascend OR Bass to descend $\hat{5} \nearrow \hat{1}$ $\hat{5} \searrow \hat{1}$

1. a) Following the example in the first cadence, on the lines beside each Authentic Cadence, write the Scale Degree Numbers for each chord to show the Voice Leading. Use arrows to indicate each direction (up $\nearrow$; down $\searrow$; or common note $\to$).
   b) Indicate whether each Chord is Complete or Incomplete.

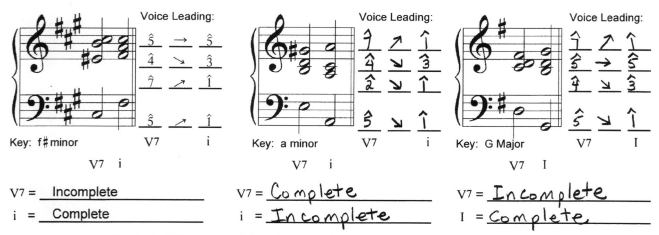

TRITONE RESOLUTION in a DOMINANT SEVENTH to TONIC CADENCE - in CHORALE (SATB) STYLE
(Use after Advanced Rudiments Page 82)

Composers will write the Authentic Cadences from a Dominant Seventh to Tonic Chord in Keyboard Style and in Chorale (SATB) Style. At this level, both the Dominant Seventh Chord and the Tonic Chord will be written in Root Position (with the root notes in the Bass Voice).

The interval (distance) in the Dominant Seventh Chord between the Leading Tone (Scale Degree $\hat{7}$) and the Subdominant (Scale Degree $\hat{4}$) is called a **Tritone**.

♫ **Ti-Do Tip:** A Tritone will be an interval of an **Augmented 4th** or a **diminished 5th**.

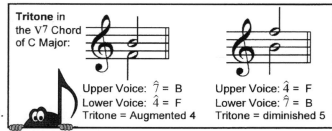

Tritone in the V7 Chord of C Major:

Upper Voice: $\hat{7}$ = B   Upper Voice: $\hat{4}$ = F
Lower Voice: $\hat{4}$ = F   Lower Voice: $\hat{7}$ = B
Tritone = Augmented 4   Tritone = diminished 5

In the V7 Chord:
Tendency Tone #1, the Leading Tone ($\hat{7}$), will always resolve to the Tonic ($\hat{1}$) in the Tonic Chord.
Tendency Tone #2, the Subdominant ($\hat{4}$), will always resolve to the Mediant ($\hat{3}$) in the Tonic Chord.

An **Augmented 4th Tritone** will be written with the Leading Tone (Scale Degree $\hat{7}$) in the Upper Voice of the Dominant Seventh Chord and the Subdominant (Scale Degree $\hat{4}$) in the Lower Voice.

A **diminished 5th Tritone** will be written with the Subdominant (Scale Degree $\hat{4}$) in the Upper Voice of the Dominant Seventh Chord and the Leading Tone (Scale Degree $\hat{7}$) in the Lower Voice.

Soprano
Alto

Tenor
Bass

Tritone Resolution
Upper Voice: Soprano: $\hat{7}$ - $\hat{1}$ Alto: $\hat{4}$ - $\hat{3}$
Lower Voice: Tenor: $\hat{4}$ - $\hat{3}$ Tenor: $\hat{7}$ - $\hat{1}$
Tritone Interval: E - A♯ = Aug 4   A♯ - E = dim 5

1. The following V7 to i Authentic Cadences are in the key of g minor. Following the example:
   a) Identify the Voices (Soprano, Alto or Tenor) and Scale Degree Resolution of the Tritone:
      Scale Degrees $\hat{7}$ - $\hat{1}$ and Scale Degrees $\hat{4}$ - $\hat{3}$.
   b) Draw arrows to show the resolution of the Tritone (Leading Tone - Tonic, and Subdominant - Mediant).
   c) Identify the notes and the interval of the Tritone.

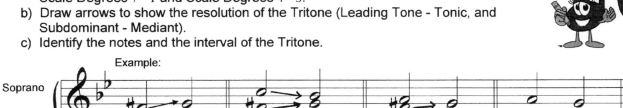

Example:

Soprano
Alto

Tenor
Bass

Tritone Resolution

Upper Voice:	Soprano: $\hat{7}$ - $\hat{1}$	Soprano: $\hat{4}$ - $\hat{3}$	Alto: $\hat{7}$ - $\hat{1}$	Alto: $\hat{4}$ - $\hat{3}$
Lower Voice:	Tenor: $\hat{4}$ - $\hat{3}$	Alto: $\hat{7}$ - $\hat{1}$	Tenor: $\hat{4}$ - $\hat{3}$	Tenor: $\hat{7}$ - $\hat{1}$
Tritone Interval:	C - F♯ = Aug 4	F♯ - C = dim 5	C - F♯ Aug 4	F♯ - C dim 5

TRITONE RESOLUTION - DOMINANT 7TH to TONIC CADENCES in KEYBOARD & CHORALE STYLE
(Use after Advanced Rudiments Page 82)

When writing a Dominant Seventh to Tonic Cadence (an Authentic Cadence) in Keyboard Style or in Chorale Style, determine which chord will be written in Complete Form and which chord will be Incomplete.

An **Incomplete** Dominant Seventh Chord ($\hat{5}$, $\hat{5}$, $\hat{7}$, $\hat{4}$) will resolve to a **Complete** Tonic Chord ($\hat{1}$, $\hat{1}$, $\hat{3}$, $\hat{5}$).

A **Complete** Dominant Seventh Chord ($\hat{5}$, $\hat{7}$, $\hat{2}$, $\hat{4}$) will resolve to an **Incomplete** Tonic Chord ($\hat{1}$, $\hat{1}$, $\hat{1}$, $\hat{3}$).

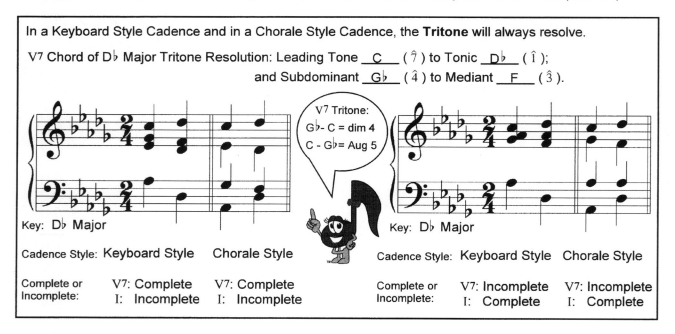

In a Keyboard Style Cadence and in a Chorale Style Cadence, the **Tritone** will always resolve.

V7 Chord of D♭ Major Tritone Resolution: Leading Tone __C__ ($\hat{7}$) to Tonic __D♭__ ($\hat{1}$);
and Subdominant __G♭__ ($\hat{4}$) to Mediant __F__ ($\hat{3}$).

V7 Tritone:
G♭- C = dim 4
C - G♭ = Aug 5

Key: D♭ Major

Cadence Style: Keyboard Style   Chorale Style

Complete or Incomplete: V7: Complete   V7: Complete
                          I: Incomplete   I: Incomplete

Key: D♭ Major

Cadence Style: Keyboard Style   Chorale Style

Complete or Incomplete: V7: Incomplete   V7: Incomplete
                          I: Complete   I: Complete

1. The following Keyboard Style and Chorale Style V7 to I are in A Major. For each cadence:
    a) Identify the notes of the Tritone Resolution (the V7 Chord note to Tonic Chord note resolutions).
    b) Add the missing notes of the V7 Chord Tritone so that they resolve to the correct Tonic Chord notes.
    c) Identify the Style of the Cadence as Keyboard or Chorale.
    d) Identify the notes in the V7 Chord and in the I Chord as Complete or Incomplete.

V7 Chord of A Major Tritone Resolution: Leading Tone __G♯__ ($\hat{7}$) to Tonic __A__ ($\hat{1}$);
and Subdominant __D__ ($\hat{4}$) to Mediant __C♯__ ($\hat{3}$).

Cadence Style: _Chorale_   _Keyboard_   _Chorale_   _Keyboard_

Complete or Incomplete: V7: _Complete_   V7: _Incomplete_   V7: _Incomplete_   V7: _Incomplete_
                          I: _Incomplete_   I: _Complete_   I: _Complete_   I: _Complete_

WRITING DOMINANT SEVENTH to TONIC CADENCES in CHORALE STYLE
(Use after Advanced Rudiments Page 82)

There is more than one correct answer (progression) for writing a Dominant 7th to Tonic Cadence.

When writing the cadence in Chorale Style, observe the: Standard Singing (Vocal) Range for each voice; Standard Interval Distances between the voices; Stem and Dot Placement Rules for Chorale (SATB) voices.

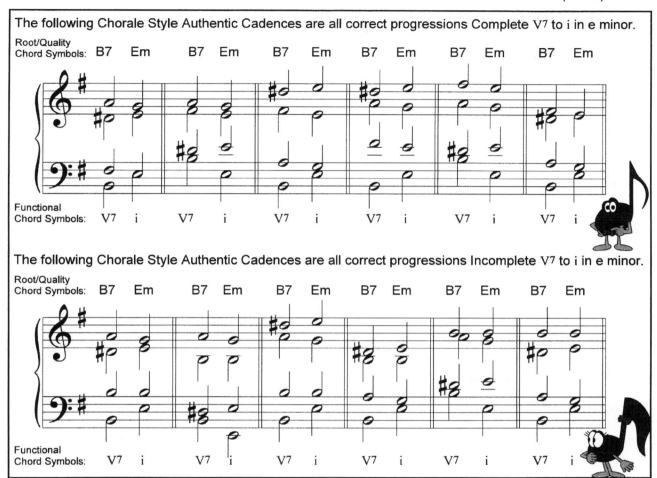

The following Chorale Style Authentic Cadences are all correct progressions Complete V7 to i in e minor.

The following Chorale Style Authentic Cadences are all correct progressions Incomplete V7 to i in e minor.

1. a) Write V7 to i Authentic Cadences in b minor. Use Chorale Style. Use a Key Signature and any necessary accidentals. Use half notes. Write a different Chord Progression in each measure. (There will be more than one correct answer.) *(one possible answer for each below)*
   b) Write the Root/Quality Chord Symbols above the staff and the Functional Chord Symbols below.

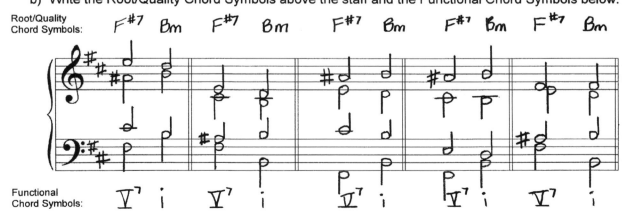

MELODIC FRAGMENTS & CADENCES - KEYBOARD STYLE (Use after Advanced Rudiments Page 82)

In a Melodic Fragment ending with a Keyboard Style Cadence, the melody given will be the Soprano voice.

So-La Says: In Keyboard Style, the stems for the Soprano Voice melody notes will follow the **Stem Rule**. **One rest** is used for the silent harmony line in the Bass Staff.

The stem direction of each Cadence Chord in the Treble Staff will be based upon the direction of the stem for the note furthest away from the middle line.

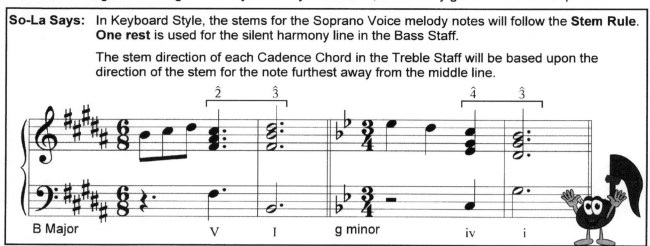

The given Soprano Voice must remain as the Soprano (top) voice when adding notes to form a Keyboard (or Chorale) style Cadence. Always add the notes **below the given notes** (the Soprano voice).

For a Keyboard Style Cadence, as the stem direction of the given note may not be altered, it is acceptable to have a competed chord with an incorrect stem direction (not following the stem rule).

♫ **Ti-Do Tip:** A Cadence is a point of rest. End a Half Cadence with V, not the V7 (an active chord).

1. Write a Keyboard Style Cadence below the bracketed melody notes. Use the correct note values. Write the Functional Chord Symbol below each chord. Name the type of Cadence (Authentic, Half or Plagal).

a) Key of d minor.

Functional
Chord Symbols: iv   i   V   i
Cadence Type: Plagal   Authentic

b) Key of F Major.

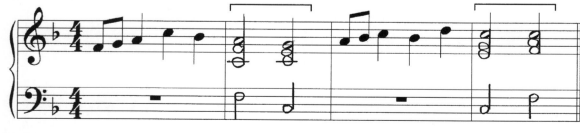

Functional
Chord Symbols: I   V   V   I
Cadence Type: Half   Authentic

MELODIC FRAGMENTS & CADENCES - CHORALE STYLE (Use after Advanced Rudiments Page 82)

In a Melodic Fragment ending with a Chorale Style Cadence, the melodic line (the given melody) will be for the Soprano Voice with the Cadence notes - stems up. A Chorale Style Cadence is written in a specific way.

So-La Says: A Chorale Style Cadence is written in the SAME way for both Keyboard Style and Chorale Style melodies. The Soprano Voice of a cadence uses notes with stems pointing up.

Keyboard Style Melody follows the "Stem Rules" (stems down for notes on or above the middle line, stems up for notes below the middle line).

Chorale Style Melody follows the "Chorale SATB Stem Rules" (stems up for Soprano and Tenor; stems down for Alto and Bass).

Soprano - Given melody notes (Stem Rules, except for Cadence)
Alto - No rest given (Treble Staff)
Tenor and Bass - One rest written for BOTH (Bass Staff)
Cadence - All voices follow the "SATB Stem Rules"

Soprano - Given melody notes (SATB Stem Rules)
Alto - One rest written below the Soprano (Treble Staff)
Tenor and Bass - One rest written for BOTH (Bass Staff)
Cadence - All voices follow the "SATB Stem Rules"

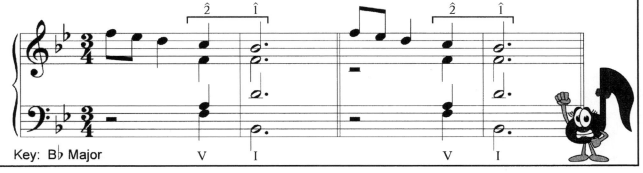

Key: B♭ Major

1. Write a Chorale Style Cadence below the bracketed melody notes. Use the correct note values. Write the Functional Chord Symbol below each chord. Name the type of Cadence (Authentic, Half or Plagal).

a) Chorale Style Melody in the key of d minor, use the "SATB Stem Rules" to complete the cadences.

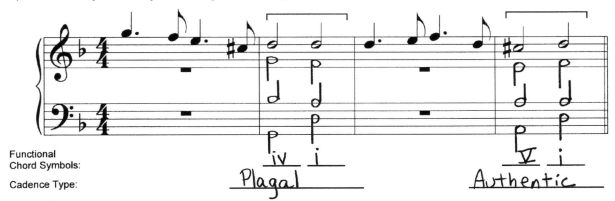

Functional
Chord Symbols: iv i   V i

Cadence Type: Plagal   Authentic

b) Keyboard Style Melody in the key of F Major, use the "SATB Stem Rules" to complete the cadences.

Functional
Chord Symbols: I V   V I

Cadence Type: Half   Authentic

TRIADS in SECOND INVERSION (Use after Advanced Rudiments Page 82)

The **position** of a triad (chord) in Keyboard or Chorale Style is based upon the note in the **Bass Voice**.
Root Position = Root in Bass; First Inversion = Third in Bass; Second Inversion = Fifth in Bass.

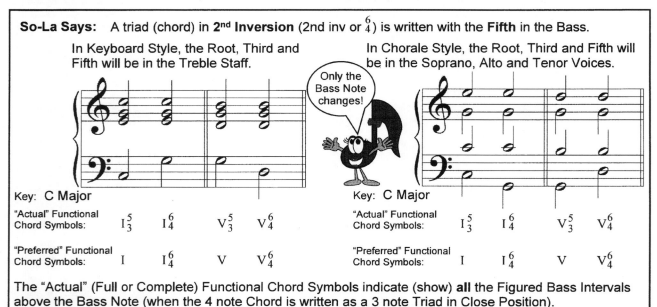

So-La Says: A triad (chord) in **2nd Inversion** (2nd inv or $^6_4$) is written with the **Fifth** in the Bass.

In Keyboard Style, the Root, Third and Fifth will be in the Treble Staff.

In Chorale Style, the Root, Third and Fifth will be in the Soprano, Alto and Tenor Voices.

Only the Bass Note changes!

The "Actual" (Full or Complete) Functional Chord Symbols indicate (show) **all** the Figured Bass Intervals above the Bass Note (when the 4 note Chord is written as a 3 note Triad in Close Position).

By changing the Bass note, a Root Position Triad (Chord) can easily be rewritten in Second Inversion.

1. Rewrite each Root Position Triad (Chord) in Second Inversion. Observe the Keyboard or Chorale Style. Write the "Actual" Functional Chord Symbol and the "Preferred" Functional Chord Symbols below.

2. Identify the Major or minor key for the Tonic and Dominant Chord in each measure. Write the "Actual" Functional Chord Symbol below each Chord (Triad) to show the Figured Bass Intervals.

THE CADENTIAL 6/4 CHORD PROGRESSION (Use after Advanced Rudiments Page 82)

Composers often write a special Chord Progression called a **Cadential 6/4 Progression** (also called a Cadential 6/4, a Cadential 6/4 to Dominant 5/3, or a Cadential 6/4 to 5/3).

A Cadential 6/4 Chord (pronounced "Cadential Six Four") is an **embellishment** (or decoration) of the Dominant Chord before it progresses to the Tonic Chord in an Authentic Cadence.

The first Chord in a Cadential 6/4 uses the same notes as the Tonic Triad in Second Inversion.

Since this Chord always progresses to a Dominant Triad in Root Position, Composers prefer to use the Functional Chord Symbols that show the **Cadential Progression of the intervals.**

Key: G Major

"Actual" Functional Chord Symbols: I_4^6 V_3^5 I_4^6 V_3^5

"Preferred" Functional Chord Symbols: V_{4-3}^{6-5} V_{4-3}^{6-5}

When writing a Cadential 6/4 Chord, the Figured Bass Numbers represent **the intervals above the Bass Note** (the Dominant). The "6/4" **does not** represent (indicate or mean) that the Dominant Triad is in Second Inversion.

The **"6/4" (six-four)** represents the notes a 6th and a 4th above the Bass Note, the Dominant. (These notes are actually the same notes as those written for the Tonic Triad in Second Inversion.)

The **"5/3" (five-three)** represents the notes a 5th and a 3rd above the Bass Note, the Dominant. (These notes are actually the same notes as those written for the Dominant Triad in Root Position.)

♫ **Ti-Do Tip:** To easily write a Cadential 6/4 to 5/3 Progression for a Dominant Chord, complete the "Cadential 6/4 Chart" by adding the note names.

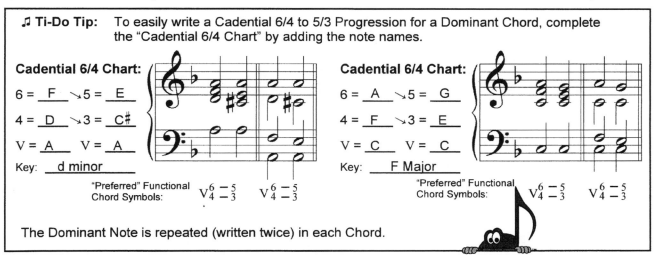

Cadential 6/4 Chart:

6 = F ↘5 = E

4 = D ↘3 = C♯

V = A   V = A

Key: d minor

"Preferred" Functional Chord Symbols: V_{4-3}^{6-5} V_{4-3}^{6-5}

Cadential 6/4 Chart:

6 = A ↘5 = G

4 = F ↘3 = E

V = C   V = C

Key: F Major

"Preferred" Functional Chord Symbols: V_{4-3}^{6-5} V_{4-3}^{6-5}

The Dominant Note is repeated (written twice) in each Chord.

---

1. a) Add the note names to complete the Cadential 6/4 Chart. Complete each Cadential 6/4 (to 5/3) Progression by adding the missing notes. Observe the Keyboard or Chorale Styles. Use half notes.
   b) Write the Functional Chord Symbols below (to show the Cadential 6/4 to 5/3 Progression).

Cadential 6/4 Chart:

6 = C♯ ↘5 = B

4 = A ↘3 = G♯

V = E   V = E

Key: A Major

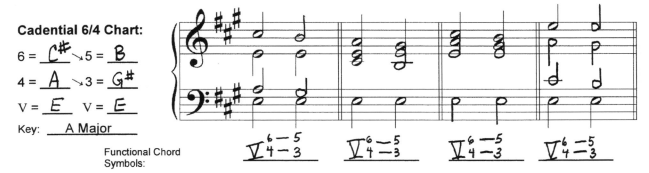

Functional Chord Symbols: V_{4-3}^{6-5} V_{4-3}^{6-5} V_{4-3}^{6-5} V_{4-3}^{6-5}

CADENTIAL 6/4 AUTHENTIC CADENCE PROGRESSION (Use after Advanced Rudiments Page 82)

A **Cadential 6/4 Chord** is a Complete Tonic Chord over a Dominant Note.

A Cadential 6/4 Chord contains 2 Dominant ($\hat{5}$) Notes, 1 Tonic ($\hat{1}$) Note and 1 Mediant ($\hat{3}$) Note.

A Cadential 6/4 Chord (the "6/4") progresses to a Complete Dominant Chord (the "5/3"), that contains 2 Dominant ($\hat{5}$) Notes, 1 Leading Tone ($\hat{7}$) Note (raised in a minor key) and 1 Supertonic ($\hat{2}$) Note.

A **Cadential 6/4 Authentic Cadence** is a progression of $V^6_4 - {}^5_3$ to I (or i in a minor key).

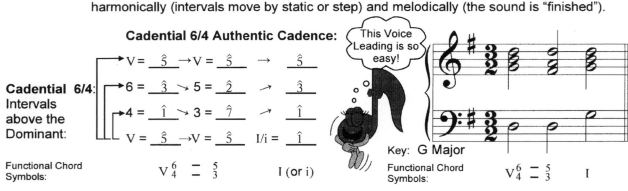

So-La Says: A **Cadential 6/4 Authentic Cadence** creates a final cadence progression that is pleasing harmonically (intervals move by static or step) and melodically (the sound is "finished").

Cadential 6/4 Authentic Cadence:

Cadential 6/4: Intervals above the Dominant:

V = $\hat{5}$ → V = $\hat{5}$ → $\hat{5}$
6 = $\hat{3}$ ↘ 5 = $\hat{2}$ ↗ $\hat{3}$
4 = $\hat{1}$ ↘ 3 = $\hat{7}$ ↗ $\hat{1}$
V = $\hat{5}$ → V = $\hat{5}$ I/i = $\hat{1}$

This Voice Leading is so easy!

Key: G Major

Functional Chord Symbols: $V^6_4 - {}^5_3$ I (or i)

Functional Chord Symbols: $V^6_4 - {}^5_3$ I

Voice Leading in a **Cadential 6/4 Authentic Cadence** in **Keyboard and Chorale Style**:

The Dominant V ($\hat{5}$) is repeated (static, written three times) as the Common Note (stasis) in all 3 Chords.

The Mediant ($\hat{3}$) steps down to the Supertonic ($\hat{2}$), then steps back up to the Mediant ($\hat{3}$).

The Tonic ($\hat{1}$) steps down to the Leading Tone ($\hat{7}$), then steps back up to the Tonic ($\hat{1}$).

The Bass Dominant ($\hat{5}$) Voice/Note will either step down to the Tonic ($\hat{1}$) Voice/Note (contrary motion) or it will step up to the Tonic (to keep the interval between the Tenor and Bass Voices a 12th or less).

A Cadential 6/4 Authentic Cadence can be identified simply as an "**Authentic Cadence**".

1. Add two chords to complete each of the following Cadential 6/4 Authentic Cadences in Keyboard Style. Observe the Key Signature and the note values. Add any necessary accidentals.

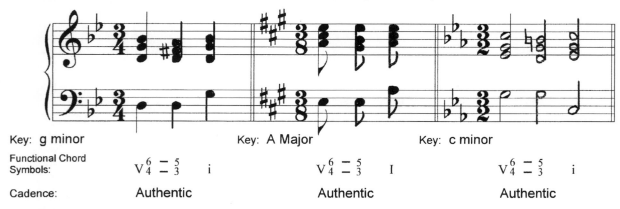

Key: g minor

Functional Chord Symbols: $V^6_4 - {}^5_3$ i

Cadence: Authentic

Key: A Major

$V^6_4 - {}^5_3$ I

Authentic

Key: c minor

$V^6_4 - {}^5_3$ i

Authentic

♫ **Ti-Do Time:** Play the above Cadential 6/4 Authentic Cadences. Observe the Voice Leading. Are the 3 voices in the Treble Staff Triad moving by same (static) and step? Is the Bass Voice within the appropriate interval range?

THE "I - IV - V$_{4-3}^{6-5}$ - I" CHORD PROGRESSION (Use after Advanced Rudiments Page 82)

A common Chord Progression used by Composers (and by musicians who are improvising, "jamming" or just having fun on their instrument) is the "Tonic, Subdominant, Dominant 6/4 - 5/3, Tonic" Progression.

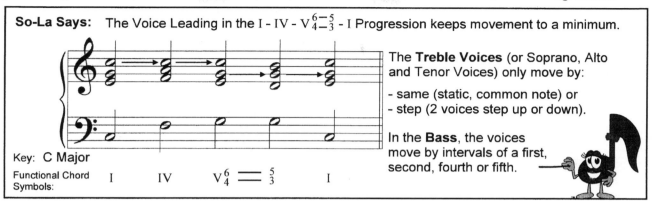

So-La Says: The Voice Leading in the I - IV - V$_{4-3}^{6-5}$ - I Progression keeps movement to a minimum.

The **Treble Voices** (or Soprano, Alto and Tenor Voices) only move by:

- same (static, common note) or
- step (2 voices step up or down).

In the **Bass**, the voices move by intervals of a first, second, fourth or fifth.

Key: C Major

Functional Chord Symbols: I   IV   V$_4^6$ ⎯ $_3^5$ I

In a **minor key**, the Progression is: i - iv - V$_{4-3}^{6-5}$ - i . The Tonic (i) and Subdominant (iv) Chords are minor; the Dominant Chord contains the raised Leading Tone (↑$\hat{7}$).

1. Name the Key for each Chord Progression. Write the Functional Chord Symbols below each chord.

Key: **B Major**

Functional Chord Symbols: I   IV   V$_{4-3}^{6-5}$ I

Key: **E♭ Major**

Functional Chord Symbols: I   IV   V$_{4-3}^{6-5}$ I

Key: **e♭ minor**

Functional Chord Symbols: i   iv   V$_{4-3}^{6-5}$ i

Key: **f♯ minor**

Functional Chord Symbols: i   iv   V$_{4-3}^{6-5}$ i

♫ **Ti-Do Time:**   Play the above Chord Progressions on your Instrument. Play them in different keys.

Improvise! Play using different rhythms, note values and articulation.
Play the chords in Broken and/or Solid Form.

Use your Whiteboard to write out your favorite I-IV-V$_{4-3}^{6-5}$-I improvisation.

Take a picture and email it to us at info@ultimatemusictheory.com.

FORM and ANALYSIS - IDENTIFYING HARMONIC PROGRESSIONS
(Use after Advanced Rudiments Page 119)

Review Pages 50 to 53 of the **Ultimate Music Theory LEVEL 7 Supplemental Workbook**:
Analysis - Non-Chord Tones, Chord Symbols, Harmonic Progression & Harmonic Rhythm.

Harmonic Progressions form the structure and design of a musical composition. Composers use chord progressions as building blocks, using different tonalities, textures, melodic figurations (musical figure - short succession of notes), pitch, rhythm, and motive (motif - states the musical idea to be developed).

A Harmonic Progression (or chord progression) is a series of chord changes that can establish a tonality. A chord change may contribute to the rhythm, meter and musical form of a piece. A chord may be built on any scale degree. Diatonic harmonization of a Maj/min scale can be based on 3 primary chords: I/i, IV/iv, V/7.

So-La Says: Use these 3 Simple Steps to Identify Chords in a Harmonic Progression:

Step #1: Name the key. (Identify if any accidentals are the raised 7th of the harmonic minor key.)
Step #2: Draw a Chord Chart. Identify the note names of the 3 primary chords (I/i, IV/iv, V/V7).
Step #3: Identify the Chords using Functional and/or Root Quality Chord Symbols.

A Chord may be written as broken chord tones (single notes) using chord notes implied by the melody.

♫ **Ti-Do Tip:**   Observe the non-chord tones. Circle the passing tone (pt) or neighbor tone (nt) notes.

1. Analyze each of the following melodies: a) Name the key. Complete the Chord Chart with the Chord Tones. b) Following the Harmonic Rhythm, write the Root/Quality Chord Symbol (in Root Position) above and the Functional Chord Symbol (in Root Position) below the Treble Staff.
   c) Circle and label any non-chord tones.

A **Harmonic Rhythm** may move more quickly approaching a cadence at the end of a phrase.

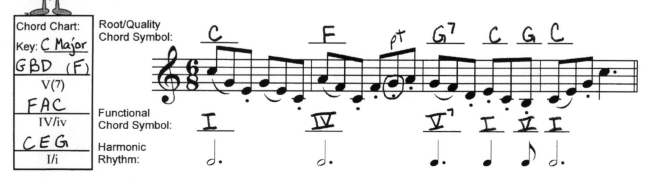

FORM and ANALYSIS - IDENTIFYING HARMONIC PROGRESSIONS - ONE, TWO, THREE
(Use after Advanced Rudiments Page 119)

A Harmonic Progression may be indicated by broken chords played as accompaniment or as two or more chord tones played together (melody & accompaniment, four part texture in keyboard style or chorale style).

So-La Says: A melody may suggest a One, Two, Three or Multi-chord Harmonic Progression. A Chord, played solid (two or more notes) or broken, will contain chord notes implied by the melody.

One-chord harmonic foundation uses I/i, and is the simplest. A repeated single chord based on the Tonic. (Are You Sleeping? *Frère Jacques* by Jean-Philippe Rameau)

Two-chord harmonic progression uses I/i, V, and is the most basic. It consists of the alternation between the Tonic, Dominant and added 7th. (*Mary Had a Little Lamb* and *Ode to Joy* by Beethoven)

Three-chord harmonic progression uses I/i, IV/iv, V/V7, and is the most common. Variations in the order of the chord progressions may be used in a four-measure phrase laying the foundation for phrase endings with a Plagal, Half or Authentic Cadence. (*Happy Birthday and Twinkle Twinkle Little Star*) Usually the only time chord V(7) goes to IV occurs when IV proceeds to I as a Plagal Progression V(7)-IV/iv- I/i.

Multi-chord harmonic progression may use any of the 7 diatonic chords. This allows for chromaticism, modulation and harmonic transition. (*Petrushka* by Igor Stravinsky)

♫ **Ti-Do Tip:**   Create a chord chart on your whiteboard. Observe the non-chord tones.

1. Identify the Harmonic Progression for each melody. a) Name the key. b) Write the Functional Chord Symbol directly below each measure. c) Label each cadence as Authentic, Half or Plagal.

2. Rewrite the Chorale Style chords from (ii) above as Root Position chords in Close Position. Use dotted half notes. Write the Root/Quality Chord Symbol above each chord.

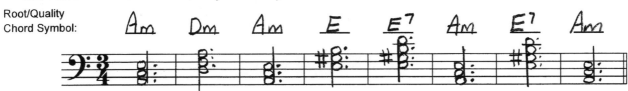

FORM and ANALYSIS - REPETITION, IMITATION, INVERSION, SEQUENCE and AUGMENTATION
(Use after Advanced Rudiments Page 127)

A Melody has a motive (short melodic and/or rhythmic idea) that is usually presented at the beginning of a composition. The motive's purpose is to provide unity, variety, relationship and fluency to the musical fabric. A motive may be altered using various composing techniques to create interest while maintaining logic.

So-La Says: A phrase is a group of notes that express a melodic idea and may be used to construct complete melodies. A phrase must end with a cadence in order to be considered a phrase. A motive may be developed through various types of alteration:

Repetition - the motive is repeated exactly, in the same voice (same rhythm, same pitch).

Imitation - immediate repetition of the motive in a different voice (same or different pitch).

Inversion - direction of each interval in the motive is reversed (repeated upside down).

Sequence - 2 or more consecutive repetitions of the motive in the same voice (higher or lower pitch).

Augmentation - rhythmic value of notes in the motive are increased (often doubled in time value).

---

1. Analyze the following musical excerpt by answering the questions below.

a) Name the Key. ___F Major___ Add the correct Time Signature directly below the bracket.

b) Identify the type of melodic motive alteration used in the RH of mm. 1 - 3. ___Sequence___

c) Circle if the rhythmic pattern in mm. 1 - 3 is: (same) or similar or different.

d) Write the Root/Quality Chord Symbol on the lines above the staff for the chords (directly) below.

e) Circle if the texture of this piece is: monophonic or (homophonic) or polyphonic.

f) Circle if the motion of the melodic pattern in m. 5 is: parallel motion or (contrary motion.)

g) Circle if the type of Cadence at letter A is: Authentic or (Half) or Plagal.

h) In m. 11, circle and label all the non-chord tones as "pt" or "nt".

i) Circle if the motion of the melodic pattern in m. 11 is: (parallel motion) or contrary motion.

j) Circle if the type of Cadence at letter B is: (Authentic) or Half or Plagal.

FORM and ANALYSIS - HOMOPHONIC, HOMORHYTHMIC and POLYPHONIC, POLYRHYTHMIC
(Use after Advanced Rudiments Page 127)

Musical Texture (melodic, harmonic and rhythmic) refers to the number of musical layers and types of layers used in a composition, and how these layers are related to each other in the music.

> **So-La Says:** A melody may be based on a monophonic texture (single melodic line, no accompaniment), and a monorhythmic texture (single rhythmic pattern). Layering creates complexity.
>
> **Homophonic Texture** - a single melodic line and harmonic accompaniment.
>
> **Homorhythmic Texture** - sameness of rhythm (similar) in both melody and harmony.
>
> **Polyphonic Texture** - two or more independent melodic lines performing simultaneously.
>
> **Polyrhythmic Texture** - two or more conflicting cross-rhythms performing simultaneously.

1. Analyze the excerpt (Morning Prayer Op. 39 No. 1 by Tchaikovsky) by answering the questions below.

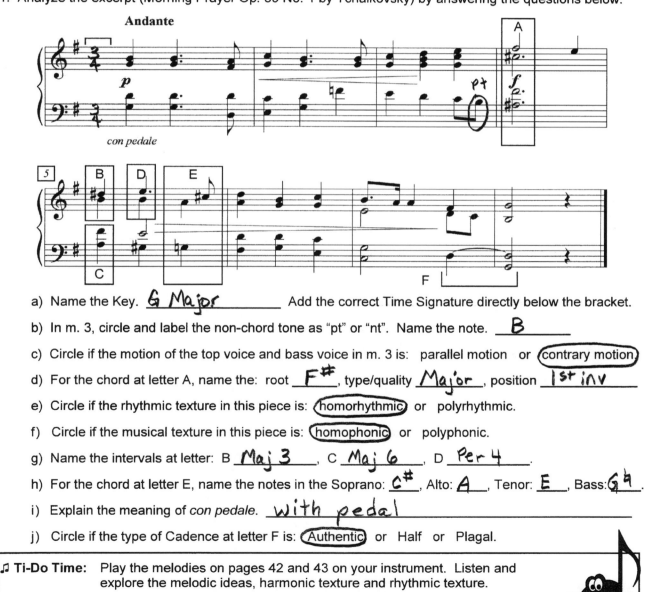

a) Name the Key. __G Major__   Add the correct Time Signature directly below the bracket.

b) In m. 3, circle and label the non-chord tone as "pt" or "nt". Name the note. __B__

c) Circle if the motion of the top voice and bass voice in m. 3 is: parallel motion or (contrary motion)

d) For the chord at letter A, name the: root __F#__, type/quality __Major__, position __1st inv__

e) Circle if the rhythmic texture in this piece is: (homorhythmic) or polyrhythmic.

f) Circle if the musical texture in this piece is: (homophonic) or polyphonic.

g) Name the intervals at letter: B __Maj 3__, C __Maj 6__, D __Per 4__.

h) For the chord at letter E, name the notes in the Soprano: __C#__, Alto: __A__, Tenor: __E__, Bass: __G♮__.

i) Explain the meaning of *con pedale*. __with pedal__

j) Circle if the type of Cadence at letter F is: (Authentic) or Half or Plagal.

> ♫ **Ti-Do Time:** Play the melodies on pages 42 and 43 on your instrument. Listen and explore the melodic ideas, harmonic texture and rhythmic texture.

FORM and ANALYSIS - MUSICAL TERMS and SIGNS (Use after Advanced Rudiments Page 138)

Musical Terms and Signs are often indicated by the Composer, giving specific direction to the performer. Understanding the meaning of the terms helps the performer interpret how the music is to be played.

♫ **Ti-Do Tip:** Observe the specific Terms and Signs for stringed instruments. The two usual ways of playing a stringed instrument are: bowed or plucked.

pizzicato - pluck the strings

arco - resume bowing after a *pizzicato* passage

❟ *breath mark* means take a breath, and/or a slight pause or lift.

⊓ *down bow* means, on a bowed string instrument, play the note while drawing the bow downward.

⋁ *up bow* means, on a bowed string instrument, play the note while drawing the bow upward.

Violin

Viola

Cello

Double Bass

This excerpt (passage or segment) from "The Happy Farmer" by Robert Schumann is notated for violin.

1. Identify and explain the music sign at each of the following letters:

   a) At the letter A: _Up bow— play the note drawing the bow upward_

   b) At the letter B: _down bow — play the note drawing the bow downward_

   c) At the letter C: _breath mark — take a breath, slight pause or lift_

So-La Says: Review the Musical Terms and Signs in the Advanced Rudiments Workbook Lesson 12. Use the 80 Free Flashcards included in the back of the book.

Articulation, Signs, Terms, Tempo, Changes in Tempo, Dynamics and Stylistic (Style in Performance). Terms, traditionally in Italian, may also be written in French, German, English or other languages.

2. Write the definition for each of the combined Musical Terms below. (*und, et, e, ed,* all mean "and")

   a) *langsam und mit Ausdruck*: _slow and with expression_

   b) *lentement et léger*: _slowly and lightly_

   c) *stringendo ed agitato*: _pressing, becoming faster and agitated_

   d) *bewegt sehr schnell*: _moving, very fast_

   e) *con sordino ed pizzicato*: _with mute and pluck the strings_

FORM and ANALYSIS - TYPES of MOTION in MUSIC (Use after Advanced Rudiments Page 138)

Melodic motion is the movement of pitches or notes in a melody. Three types of melodic movements are: conjunct (movement by step), disjunct (movement by skip - interval of a 3rd; leap - interval larger than a 3rd) or static (note repetition before movement).

Motion in Music refers to the direction(s) of movement between two different voices. Five types of motion in music between voices are: parallel, similar, contrary, static (*stasis*) and oblique.

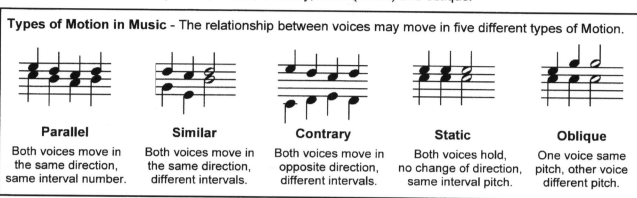

Parallel	**Similar**	**Contrary**	**Static**	**Oblique**
Both voices move in the same direction, same interval number.	Both voices move in the same direction, different intervals.	Both voices move in opposite direction, different intervals.	Both voices hold, no change of direction, same interval pitch.	One voice same pitch, other voice different pitch.

♫ **Ti-Do Tip:** Terms written in different languages can have the same definition (such as moderate tempo).

German term	*mässig* or *mäßig*	moderate tempo
French term	*modéré*	moderate tempo
Italian term	*moderato*	moderate tempo

Glissando, gliss. is the motion of a continuous slide upward or downward between two or more pitches.

Signs in music can be written to indicate specific direction.

glissando, gliss. - Continuous slide upward (⟋) between 2 or more pitches.

glissando, gliss. - Continuous slide downward (⟍) between 2 or more pitches.

1. Analyze the following piece by answering the questions below.

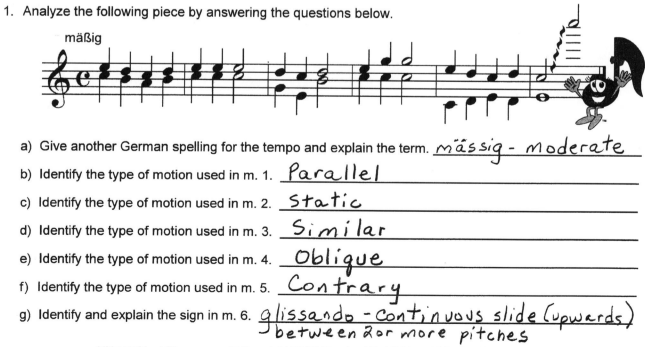

a) Give another German spelling for the tempo and explain the term. <u>mässig - moderate</u>

b) Identify the type of motion used in m. 1. <u>Parallel</u>

c) Identify the type of motion used in m. 2. <u>Static</u>

d) Identify the type of motion used in m. 3. <u>Similar</u>

e) Identify the type of motion used in m. 4. <u>Oblique</u>

f) Identify the type of motion used in m. 5. <u>Contrary</u>

g) Identify and explain the sign in m. 6. <u>glissando - continuous slide (upwards) between 2 or more pitches</u>

ANALYSIS - UNACCENTED NON-CHORD TONES - PASSING TONES and NEIGHBOR TONES
(Use after Advanced Rudiments Page 138)

A melody is a combination of a melodic contour (notes moving by step, skip, leap or repeat) and rhythm.
A melody may move from one chord tone to another chord tone or move by step into a non-chord tone.

A **Non-Chord Tone**, or non-harmonic note, is a note that does not belong to the chord (I/i , IV/iv, V/V7).
A non-chord tone can move by half step (diatonic or chromatic) or whole step connecting two chord tones.

So-La Says: **Non-Chord Tone** (a step between 2 chord tones) may be a passing tone or a neighbor tone.
An "unaccented" Non-Chord Tone falls on a weak beat or weak part (subdivision) of a beat.

Passing tone "pt" is a non-chord tone moving by step (same direction), connecting two chord tones.
Neighbor tone "nt" is a non-chord tone moving by step (up or down), adjacent to a returning chord tone.

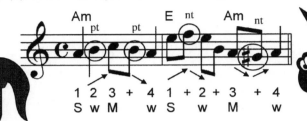

Am a minor Chord Tones: A - C - E
i   Non-Chord Notes: G# - B - D - F

Dm d minor Chord Tones: D - F - A
iv Non-Chord Notes: C - E - G# - B

E   E Major Chord Tones: E - G# - B
V   Non-Chord Notes: D - F - A - C

Key: a minor, harmonic scale A B C D E F G# A
Chord Tones are based on the notes of the scale.

♫ **Ti-Do Tip:**   Passing tone "pt" bridge - SAME direction.   Neighbor tone "nt" bump - UP or DOWN direction.

1. For each melody: a) Name the key. b) Write the Root/Quality Chord Symbols (in root pos) on the lines above each staff. c) Write the Functional Chord Symbols (in root pos) on the lines below each staff.
   d) Circle and label the non-chord tones as "pt" for passing tone or "nt" for neighbor tone above each note.

REWRITING A MELODY - MINOR KEYS ADDING NON-CHORD TONES
(Use after Advanced Rudiments Page 138)

A melody may be written in a Major key or in a minor key using the notes based on the scale. A melody written in a minor key may be based on the natural minor, harmonic minor or melodic minor scale. A melody may use primary chord tones (I/i, IV/iv and V) and non-chord tones for melodic decoration of chord tones.

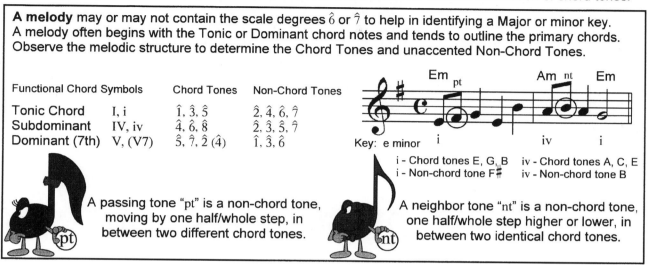

A melody may or may not contain the scale degrees $\hat{6}$ or $\hat{7}$ to help in identifying a Major or minor key. A melody often begins with the Tonic or Dominant chord notes and tends to outline the primary chords. Observe the melodic structure to determine the Chord Tones and unaccented Non-Chord Tones.

Functional Chord Symbols		Chord Tones	Non-Chord Tones
Tonic Chord	I, i	$\hat{1}, \hat{3}, \hat{5}$	$\hat{2}, \hat{4}, \hat{6}, \hat{7}$
Subdominant	IV, iv	$\hat{4}, \hat{6}, \hat{8}$	$\hat{2}, \hat{3}, \hat{5}, \hat{7}$
Dominant (7th)	V, (V7)	$\hat{5}, \hat{7}, \hat{2} (\hat{4})$	$\hat{1}, \hat{3}, \hat{6}$

Key: e minor

i - Chord tones E, G, B iv - Chord tones A, C, E
i - Non-chord tone F♯ iv - Non-chord tone B

A passing tone "pt" is a non-chord tone, moving by one half/whole step, in between two different chord tones.

A neighbor tone "nt" is a non-chord tone, one half/whole step higher or lower, in between two identical chord tones.

♫ **Ti-Do Tip:**   For melodies without a Bass voice, Root/Quality Chord Symbols are written as Root Position.

1. For each melody: a) Name the key. b) Write the Root/Quality and Functional Chord Symbol on each line.
   c) Rewrite the melody adding non-chord tones. When adding non-chord tones, change the given quarter note to an 8th note followed by an 8th note passing tone or neighbor tone. Circle and label the pt/nt.
   (one possible answer for each below)

MELODY WRITING - MINOR KEYS - AVOID AUG 2 (Use after Advanced Rudiments Page 144)

A Melody is usually written with a Key Signature that identifies the Major and relative minor key. A melody is based on the diatonic notes of the scale. In a minor key, the scale may be: natural, harmonic (raised 7th), melodic (raised/lowered 6th and 7th), or a combination, moving from one minor scale type to another.

So-La Says: A Melody in a minor key may contain accidentals for the raised 6th and/or 7th degree notes.

A minor key usually contains the raised 7th of the harmonic minor in a V - I progression. The dissonant Aug 2 (between the $\hat{6}$ - $\hat{7}$ scale degrees of the harmonic minor) was usually avoided in melodies in Western Music (1600 - present). In an ascending or descending scale passage of a melody, the Aug 2 is converted into a Maj 2 using the appropriate form of the melodic minor scale ($\hat{6}$ - $\hat{7}$ - interval of a Maj 2).

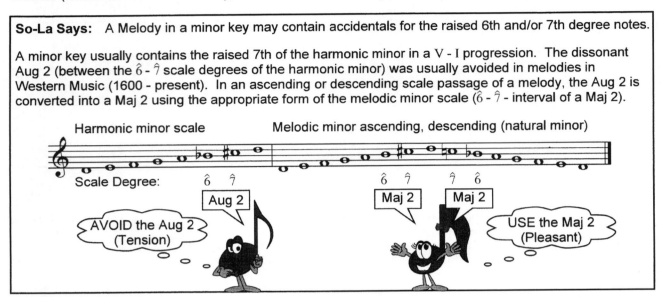

♫ **Ti-Do Tip:**   A Melody in a minor key is identified simply as a minor key, not natural, harmonic or melodic.

1. Sing or play each melody and listen for the Aug 2 or Maj 2 intervals. a) Name the key. b) Write the Root/Quality Chord Symbols in root position. c) Rewrite each melody changing the Aug 2 into a Major 2 using your ear to help you decide which form of the melodic minor scale should be used. d) Circle and label the non-chord tones as "pt" or "nt". *There may be more than one "pt" in a row.

MELODY WRITING - MINOR KEYS - i, iv and V CHORDS (Use after Advanced Rudiments Page 144)

A Melody written in a minor key may or may not use the raised/lowered $\hat{6}$ and $\hat{7}$ degrees of the harmonic or melodic minor scale. The harmony supporting the melody determines which scale form to use for $\hat{6}$ and $\hat{7}$.

> ♫ **Ti-Do Tip:** Three Tips for writing a melody in a minor key.
>
> **Tip #1:** Use the Harmonic minor scale pattern (raised 7th, both ascending and descending) when a melodic line moves from $\hat{7}$ to $\hat{8}$, or $\hat{8}$ to $\hat{7}$ with a V-i or i-V chord progression.
>
> **Tip #2:** Use the Melodic minor scale pattern (raised 6th and 7th, both ascending and descending) when a melodic line passes through $\hat{6}$ and $\hat{7}$ with a V-i or i-V chord progression.
>
> **Tip #3:** Use the Natural minor scale pattern (no added accidentals, both ascending and descending) when a melodic line passes through $\hat{6}$ and $\hat{7}$ with a harmony of the iv chord (and usually i chord).
>
>
>
> Key: a minor Chord Tones: i - A, C, E iv - D, F, A V - E, G♯, B
>
> *Double melodic passing tones - when more than one passing tone in a row (moving in stepwise motion) bridges the leap between two chord tones, they are non-harmonic passing tones or embellishing tones.
>
> **Accented passing "ap" or **Accented neighbor "an" notes occur on a strong beat or strong subdivision of a beat. At this level identify all accented or unaccented passing tones as "pt" and neighbor tones as "nt".

1. For each melody: a) Name the key. b) Write the Root/Quality Chord Symbols in root position.
   c) Rewrite each melody adding chord and non-chord tones. When adding notes, change the given half notes to quarter notes or eighth notes followed by a passing tone, neighbor tone or chord tone. d) Circle and label the pt/nt. *You may use more than one "pt" in a row. (one possible answer for each below)

MELODY WRITING - MAJOR and MINOR KEYS - HARMONIC MINOR

Review Pages 54 to 59 of the **Ultimate Music Theory LEVEL 7 Supplemental Workbook**: Composing in a Major Key - Parallel Period and Contrasting Period.

A Melody can be written in a Major or minor key based on the primary chords (I/i , IV/iv, V).

A Melody in a Major key is based on the Key Signature. A Melody in a minor key is based on the Key Signature plus the accidentals of the harmonic minor and/or melodic minor (descending natural minor) scales. For melody writing in minor keys for LEVEL 8, use the KISS Method. *Keep It Super Simple!*

♩ **Ti-Do Tip:** Three Tips for writing a melody in a minor key.

Tip #1: Identify the key. Write the chord tones for the i , iv, V (raised 7th), chords. Use the UMT Whiteboard to create your chord chart.

Tip #2: Compose a melody based on the primary chords (i , iv, V). Move in stepwise motion to the final stable scale degree $\hat{1}$ (or $\hat{3}$).

Tip #3: Use both chord tones and non-chord tones. (Unaccented non-chord tones are written on the weak beat or weak subdivision of the beat).

A 4 measure phrase may end with a Half Cadence: iv-V, i-V (always end on V chord, NEVER end on V7) or an Authentic Cadence: V-i. At this level, when writing an 8 measure phrase, end the first 4 measure phrase with a Half Cadence, and end the second 4 measure phrase with an Authentic Cadence.

---

1. For each melody: a) Name the key. b) Observe the Functional Chord Symbols to complete each phrase. Use one or more non-chord tones in each melody. Circle and label them. c) Name the type of cadence.

(one possible answer for each below)

i)   i   V   i   V   i   iv   i   V

Key: a minor   Cadence: Half

ii)   I   IV   I   V   I

Key: Ab Major   Cadence: Authentic

iii)   I   V   I   V

Key: D Major   Cadence: Half

iv)   i   iv   V   i

Key: C minor   Cadence: Authentic

MELODY WRITING - MUSICAL FIGURES

Composing a melody requires a logical harmonic progression and melodic figurations (**Musical Figure** - short succession of notes) that complete a musical phrase. A musical figure may be repeated or altered.

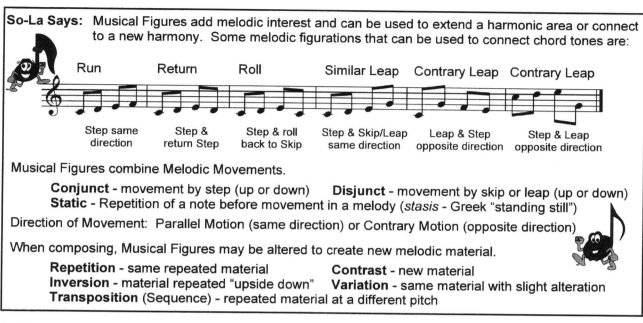

So-La Says: Musical Figures add melodic interest and can be used to extend a harmonic area or connect to a new harmony. Some melodic figurations that can be used to connect chord tones are:

Run	Return	Roll	Similar Leap	Contrary Leap	Contrary Leap
Step same direction	Step & return Step	Step & roll back to Skip	Step & Skip/Leap same direction	Leap & Step opposite direction	Step & Leap opposite direction

Musical Figures combine Melodic Movements.

Conjunct - movement by step (up or down)   **Disjunct** - movement by skip or leap (up or down)
Static - Repetition of a note before movement in a melody (*stasis* - Greek "standing still")

Direction of Movement: Parallel Motion (same direction) or Contrary Motion (opposite direction)

When composing, Musical Figures may be altered to create new melodic material.

Repetition - same repeated material   **Contrast** - new material
Inversion - material repeated "upside down"   **Variation** - same material with slight alteration
Transposition (Sequence) - repeated material at a different pitch

1. For each melody: a) Name the key. b) Observe the Functional Chord Symbols to complete each phrase. Use one or more non-chord tones in each melody. Circle and label them. c) Name the type of cadence.

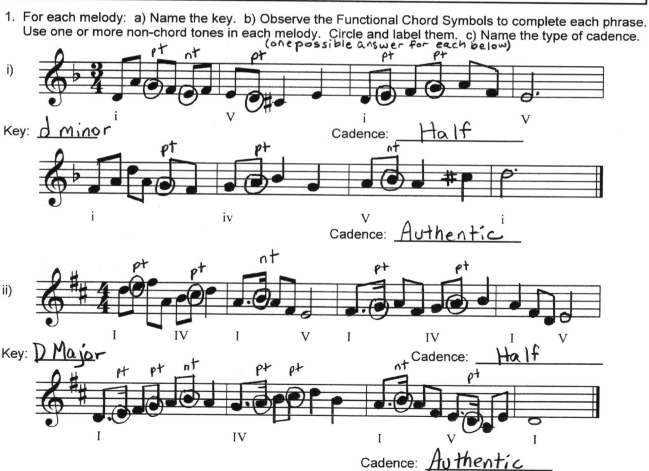

i) Key: d minor   Cadence: Half

Cadence: Authentic

ii) Key: D Major   Cadence: Half

Cadence: Authentic

COMPOSING - PARALLEL PERIOD and CONTRASTING PERIOD - MINOR KEYS

Now that you are a composer, it's time to use the **ICE** Method. **I**magine, **C**ompose, **E**xplore different ways of melody writing to complete a 2 four-measure phrase in a Parallel Period or in a Contrasting Period.

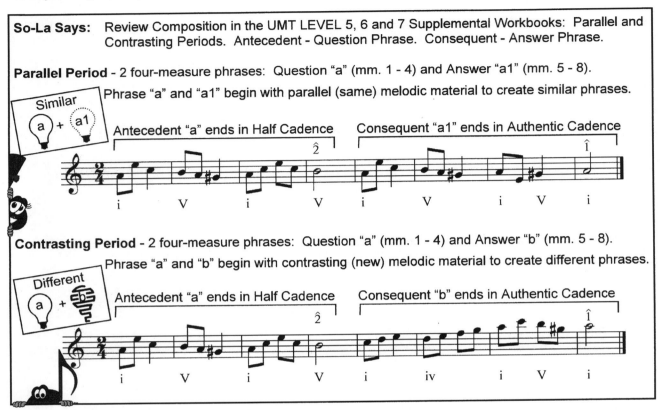

So-La Says: Review Composition in the UMT LEVEL 5, 6 and 7 Supplemental Workbooks: Parallel and Contrasting Periods. Antecedent - Question Phrase. Consequent - Answer Phrase.

Parallel Period - 2 four-measure phrases: Question "a" (mm. 1 - 4) and Answer "a1" (mm. 5 - 8).

Phrase "a" and "a1" begin with parallel (same) melodic material to create similar phrases.

Similar: a + a1

Antecedent "a" ends in Half Cadence   Consequent "a1" ends in Authentic Cadence

i   V   i   V   i   V   i   V   i

Contrasting Period - 2 four-measure phrases: Question "a" (mm. 1 - 4) and Answer "b" (mm. 5 - 8).

Phrase "a" and "b" begin with contrasting (new) melodic material to create different phrases.

Different: a +

Antecedent "a" ends in Half Cadence   Consequent "b" ends in Authentic Cadence

i   V   i   V   i   iv   i   V   i

♫ **Ti-Do Tip:** In a Contrasting Period, the new contrasting melodic material "b" may use a different rhythm, melody and/or harmonic chord progression. End "b" on the Tonic, stable scale degree 1̂.

1. Name the key. Compose 2 different Answer Phrases ("b") for the given Question Phrase ("a") to create a Contrasting Period. End on stable scale degree 1̂. Write Functional Chord Symbols below each measure.

(one possible answer for each below)

"a"

Key: **a minor**

i   V   i   V

"b"

i   iv   i   V   i

"b"

i   iv   V   i

COMPOSING - CONSEQUENT "ANSWER" PHRASE - MAJOR & MINOR KEYS

When composing a **Consequent "Answer" Phrase** to an Antecedent "Question" Phrase in a Parallel or Contrasting Period, use a logical harmonic progression, melodic figurations and cadence phrase endings.

> **So-La Says:** Use these 3 Simple Steps for writing a melody in a Parallel or Contrasting Period.
>
> Use melodic and rhythmic ideas from the Question phrase to reflect the character in the Answer Phrase.
>
> **Step #1:** Outline the melody by choosing one chord tone for the beginning of each beat or new chord.
>
> **Step #2:** "Connect the dots" with eighth notes or sixteenth notes (or other rhythms), use mostly step-wise motion and leap only between chord tones. Move directly towards a goal (cadence resolution).
>
> **Step #3:** Sing or play your composition. Listen critically, revising any spots that do not sound pleasing to the ear or do not resolve to the cadence. Remember the Ti-Do Tips and *Keep It Super Simple!*

1. For each melodic opening: a) Name the key. b) Complete the Question Phrase, ending on an unstable scale degree. Compose an Answer Phrase to create a Contrasting Period, ending on a stable scale degree. c) Draw a phrase mark over each phrase (use square phrases). d) Name the type of cadence (Authentic or Half) directly below each phrase ending. *(one possible answer for each below)*

COMPOSING - CONTRASTING PERIOD - "HARMONIC ROAD MAP"

When composing a Contrasting Period in a Major or minor key with the first two measures given, begin with the Harmonic Road Map. The Harmonic Progression outlines the journey with a resting stop along the way.

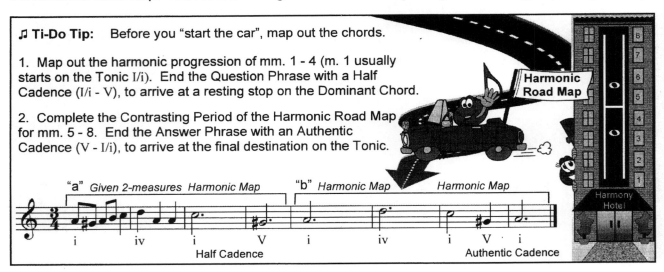

A Melody has a **Harmonic Road Map** of chords that have a relationship to one another (Primary Chords I/i, IV/iv, V). The characteristics of harmony are: tonality, progression, combined pitches (usually 3) and key. A cadence may move from one measure to another, or a cadence may resolve within the same measure.

(one possible answer for each below)

1. For each melodic opening: a) Name the key. Map out the Harmonic Progression by writing Functional Chord Symbols below each measure. b) Complete the Question Phrase, ending on an unstable scale degree. Compose an Answer Phrase to create a Contrasting Period, ending on a stable scale degree. c) Draw a phrase mark over each phrase. d) Name the type of cadences (Authentic or Half).

COMPOSING - CONTRASTING PERIOD - "MELODIC ROAD MAP"

Composing an Answer Phrase to a Question Phrase - In a Contrasting Period in a Major or minor key, with the first two measures given, follow the Harmonic Road Map to write your melodic line above the harmony.

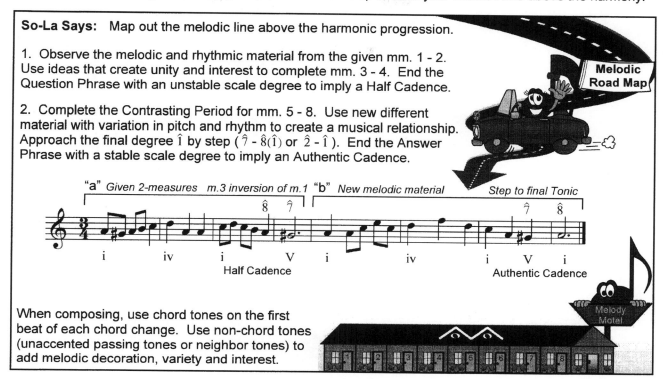

So-La Says: Map out the melodic line above the harmonic progression.

1. Observe the melodic and rhythmic material from the given mm. 1 - 2. Use ideas that create unity and interest to complete mm. 3 - 4. End the Question Phrase with an unstable scale degree to imply a Half Cadence.

2. Complete the Contrasting Period for mm. 5 - 8. Use new different material with variation in pitch and rhythm to create a musical relationship. Approach the final degree $\hat{1}$ by step ($\hat{7}$ - $\hat{8}(\hat{1})$ or $\hat{2}$ - $\hat{1}$). End the Answer Phrase with a stable scale degree to imply an Authentic Cadence.

When composing, use chord tones on the first beat of each chord change. Use non-chord tones (unaccented passing tones or neighbor tones) to add melodic decoration, variety and interest.

A Melody has a **Melodic Road Map** of tones that have a relationship to one another. The characteristics of a melody are: Range - narrow, medium or wide (lowest to highest pitch); Shape or curve - conjunct (step), disjunct (skip or leap between chord tones) or stasis (repeat) and Direction - movement (up or down).

Use your Ultimate Whiteboard (shop.UltimateMusicTheory.com) to write your melody first. Play it on your instrument. Make any necessary changes on your whiteboard, play it again. Write your final melody.

1. For the melodic opening: a) Name the key. Map out the Harmonic Progression and build the melodic line based on the chords. b) Complete the Question Phrase, ending on an unstable scale degree. Compose an Answer Phrase to create a Contrasting Period, ending on a stable scale degree. c) Draw a phrase mark over each phrase. d) Name the type of cadences (Authentic or Half). e) Title your melody. *(one possible answer below)*

COMPOSING - CONTRASTING PERIOD - MAJOR and MINOR KEYS - MAP IT OUT

Map it out! The Melodic and Rhythmic Structure of a melody is built on a Harmonic Progression.
A Harmonic Progression refers to the order of chords used in the music or implied by the melody.

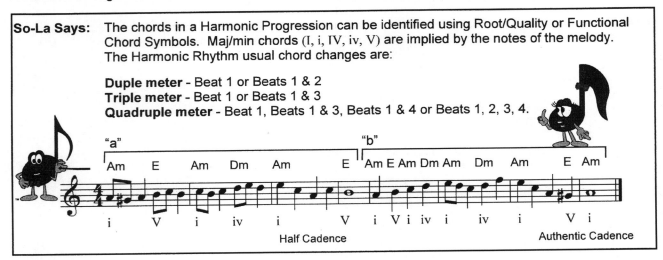

So-La Says: The chords in a Harmonic Progression can be identified using Root/Quality or Functional Chord Symbols. Maj/min chords (I, i, IV, iv, V) are implied by the notes of the melody. The Harmonic Rhythm usual chord changes are:

Duple meter - Beat 1 or Beats 1 & 2
Triple meter - Beat 1 or Beats 1 & 3
Quadruple meter - Beat 1, Beats 1 & 3, Beats 1 & 4 or Beats 1, 2, 3, 4.

♫ **Ti-Do Tip:** Creating a Chord Chart (either on your Whiteboard or in the margin before the music) makes identifying Chord Tones (the notes in each Chord) and non-chord tones (pt/nt) easy.

1. For each melodic opening: a) Name the key. B) Write the Root/Quality and Functional Chord Symbols to Map out the Harmonic Progression. c) Complete the Question Phrase, ending on an unstable scale degree to imply a Half Cadence. Compose an Answer Phrase to create a Contrasting Period, ending on a stable scale degree to imply an Authentic Cadence. d) Name the type of cadences (Authentic or Half).
(one possible answer for each below)

COMPOSING - CONTRASTING PERIOD - MAJOR and MINOR KEYS - FINAL CHECK LIST

Harmonic Progression is a series of different chords written one after the other. A Cadence is a two Chord Progression: Authentic Cadence (final cadence ends on I, i), Half Cadence (non-final cadence ends on V).

Harmonic Rhythm is the speed at which chords change in a **Harmonic Progression**. Harmonic Rhythm (harmonic tempo) is determined by the melodic line and the Time Signature. The harmonic rhythm often slows down at the end of a phrase, ending with a final or non-final cadence.

> ♫ **Ti-Do Tip:** Use the **Final Check List** to complete your melody writing in a Contrasting Period.
>
> ☑ Read the instructions carefully. Name the key. Write the primary chord note names (I/i, IV/iv, V). Write the harmonic progression map using chord symbols.
>
> ☑ Complete the melodic line with unity and variety. Add one high climax note or repeated notes. Add unaccented non-chord tones to embellish the melody.
>
> ☑ Use a variety of musical figures, moving by step, skip or leap between chord tones. Add musical ideas (sequence, inversions) that maintain the contour of the melody.
>
> ☑ End the Question phrase on an unstable scale degree implying a Half Cadence. End the Answer phrase on a stable scale degree (Tonic preferred) implying an Authentic Cadence. Sing or play your melody to review the melodic line.

1. For each melodic opening: a) Name the key. b) Complete the Question Phrase. Compose an Answer Phrase to create a Contrasting Period, ending on a stable scale degree. c) Draw a phrase mark above each phrase. d) Name the type of cadences (Authentic or Half). (one possible answer for each below)

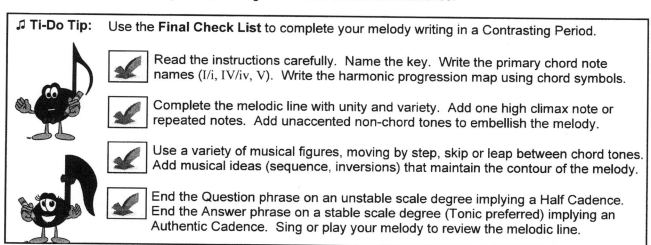

Key: g minor   Cadence: Half

Cadence: Authentic

Key: D Major   Cadence: Half

Cadence: Authentic

IMAGINE, COMPOSE, EXPLORE

♪ Imagine - Use your imagination to create a title that describes your composition.

♪ Compose - Write your composition and add your name (top right) as the composer.

♪ Explore - Add "So-La Sparkles" (terms & signs) to express how the music is played.

So-La Says:	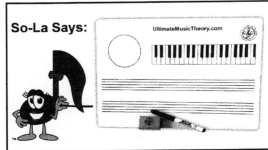	**When composing follow these 3 Composing Steps:**

1. Record your melody as you play. Use it as a reference.

2. Write your melody on the Whiteboard. Try different ideas.

3. Write your melody in the workbook. Add "So-La Sparkles" of articulation, dynamics, etc. to create your final composition.

1. Complete the following melody to create a Contrasting Period. Add a title and your name (composer).

   a) Name the key. Add the correct Time Signature directly below the bracket.
   b) Complete the Question phrase ending on an unstable scale degree.
   c) Compose an Answer phrase to create a contrasting period ending on a stable scale degree.
   d) Draw a phrase mark over each phrase (use square phrase mark brackets).
   e) Name the type of cadence (half or authentic) at the end of each phrase.
   (one possible answer below)

Bonus: Add "So-La Sparkles" (write words too) and Play!

♫ **Ti-Do Time:** Get your "Composers Certificate". SCAN your composition (on this page) and send it to us at: info@ultimatemusictheory.com and we will send you a special **Ultimate Music Theory Composers Certificate** - FREE.

ANALYSIS and SIGHT READING

Parrot Sings The Blues

Moderato, Swing!

Julianne Warkentin

1. Analyze the music by answering the questions below. Play the piece "Parrot Sings the Blues".

   a) Add the correct Time Signature directly below the bracket.

   b) Explain the term *Moderato*. <u>at a moderate tempo</u>

   c) Name the interval at letter A: <u>min 9</u>   Name both notes, lower note first: <u>B♭</u> <u>C♭</u>

   d) Circle and label a Tritone. Name the interval: <u>dim 5</u> Name both notes, lower note first: <u>A</u> <u>E♭</u>

   e) Give the total number of beats given to the tied notes at letter B. <u>1½</u> Name the note: <u>C</u>

   f) Circle the type of chord indicated at letter C as: Major or minor or (Dom 7) or dim 7.

   g) Name and explain the sign at letter D: <u>tenuto - held sustained   accent - stressed note</u>

   h) Name the interval at letter E: <u>Aug 1</u>   Name both notes, lower note first: <u>E♭</u> <u>E♮</u>

   i) Write the measure number in the box directly above line 2 & 3. Total number of measures: <u>13</u>

   j) Name and explain the sign at letter F: <u>Triplet - 3 notes played in the time of 2 notes of the same time value</u>

MUSIC HISTORY - MIDDLE AGES - MEDIEVAL ERA (*ca 476 - 1450*) - HILDEGARD VON BINGEN

In the **Medieval Era**, music was often based on the teachings of the Christian Church. Plainchant (plainsong in Latin text) was sung by a single voice or multiple voices singing in unison in monophonic texture (unaccompanied single melodic line) performed in free unmeasured rhythm (as in the spoken word).

The Medieval Plainchant (chant) was based on modes (scale patterns often called church modes) and had a unique system of notation using a staff of four lines (not five lines as in modern notation) and NO bar lines.

Music, notated in Neumes, were symbols of successive musical pitches and direction written above the text to suggest the contour of the melody, as in the Morality Play "Ordo Virtutum" by **Hildegard von Bingen**.

Hildegard von Bingen (1098 - 1179) was the tenth child of Hildebert von Bermersheim and Mechthild. She demonstrated extraordinary visionary powers by the age of 5 and, at the age of 8, she entered religious life at a Benedictine monastery (to be a nun).

Hildegard von Bingen was a brilliant woman. Not only did she become the Abbess (head of the abbey of nuns) at age 38, she was also a religious administrator, author, poet, prolific theologian, scientist, visionary mystic, healer, musician and composer..

"Music stirs our hearts and engages our souls in ways we can't describe."
~ Hildegard von Bingen

On October 7, 2012, Saint Hildegard von Bingen was named Doctor (Latin: *Doctor* means "teacher") of the Church by Pope Benedict XVI for her contribution to the growth of the Catholic Church of her time.

Plainchant (Latin: *cantus planus*) are chants with Latin texts used in the liturgies (public religious worship or ritual in a divine act). Plainchant (or Plainsong) is a modal melody in free rhythm, in monophonic texture.

Monophonic Texture (the simplest of musical textures) is a melody consisting of a single melodic line (sung or played) without accompanying harmony or chords.

Modes (developed by ancient Greeks) were used for the modal plainsong. Modes have a specific pattern of whole steps and half steps, as a Major scale beginning on a different scale degree. Modes on Major Scale degrees are: Ionian ($\hat{1}$), Dorian ($\hat{2}$), Phrygian ($\hat{3}$), Lydian ($\hat{4}$), Mixolydian ($\hat{5}$), Aeolian ($\hat{6}$) and Locrian ($\hat{7}$).

Morality Play is a genre of medieval drama and music that used allegorical (symbolic) figures to convey or teach a religious or moral idea. Roots of the morality play lie in the liturgical drama of the Catholic church.

Ordo Virtutum (Latin: *Order of the Virtues*) is a Medieval liturgical drama (text and music), an allegorical Morality Play by Hildegard of Bingen, composed c. 1151. **Performing Forces:** 17 Female Voices representing 1 Soul and 16 Virtues, plus 1 spoken Male Voice as the Devil with improvised accompaniment.

Go to **GSGMUSIC.com** - For Easy Access to listening to Hildegard von Bingen's *Ordo Virtutum*.

1. Hildegard von Bingen lived during the Musical Period (*ca 476 - 1450*) called <u>Medieval Era</u>.

2. The Plainchant was based on scale patterns called <u>modes</u> or <u>church modes</u>.

3. Hildegard von Bingen wrote a Morality Play called <u>Ordo Virtutum</u>.

4. A Morality Play features a melody with a single melodic line called <u>monophonic</u> texture.

5. The Morality Play genre used <u>allegorical (symbolic)</u> figures to convey or teach a religious or moral idea.

6. Ordo Virtutum, written in the Latin language, means <u>Order of the Virtues</u>.

7. Performing Forces of Ordo Virtutum: <u>17</u> Female Voice(s), <u>1</u> Male Voice(s) and accompaniment.

MUSIC HISTORY - HILDEGARD VON BINGEN - ORDO VIRTUTUM

Ordo Virtutum (Latin: *Order of the Virtues*) **by Hildegard von Bingen** is a Play of Virtues - Morality Play. The characters represent: a Soul (Anima and her companion lamenting Souls), 16 Virtues (Humility, Knowledge of God, World Rejection, Charity, Celestial Love, Modesty, Hope, Patience, Obedience, Innocence, Discretion, Faith, Discipline, Chastity, Victory, Compassion) and the Devil (Diabolus).

Ordo Virtutum is massive in volume with 82 melodies based on Plainchant. A short (unaccompanied) version of Ordo Virtutum is included in Hildegard's Scivias (the most famous account of her visions).

Prologue - Virtues are introduced to the Patriarchs and Prophets.

Scene 1 - Anima (the happy Soul) enters, her voice contrasts with the unhappy lamenting Souls. Anima is eager to skip life and go straight to Heaven. The Virtues tell her she must first live and battle against Diabolus (the Devil who entices her). She becomes depressed and laments too.

Scene 2 - Humility (Queen of the Virtues) and the Virtues present themselves while the Devil, Diabolus, interrupts with insults. Humilitas' call to joy is contradicted by the Virtues', who mourn for Anima.

Scene 3 - Anima returns grief stricken and calls upon the Virtues. The Virtues, seeing her as the lost sheep, lift Anima and carry her back to their dwelling. The Virtues have accepted Anima back and turn on the Devil.

Scene 4 - The Devil enters and fights to bring the Soul (Anima) down. The Soul is repentant and engages in a victorious battle to overcome the Devil.

Finale - Virtues and Souls - Praise God and give thanks.

Ordo Virtutum Scene 4: Quae es, aut unde venis? (Latin: *Who art thou, and from whence comest thou?*) The question is asked by the Devil, Diabolus, who has no music in him. He never sings, only speaks in *strepitus* (violent shouting), "*You embraced me, and I led you forth, but now by turning back you defy me.*"

The Plainchant reply is sung in monophonic texture by the penitent Soul, Anima "*I recognized that all my ways were evil, and so I escaped from you. But now, deceiver, I fight against you.*"

The Solo voices (Humility, Victory and Chastity) alternate with the Chorus voices (Virtues) sung in unison.

The connection between the emotional imagery and melodic motives are expressed in the modal melodies (not driven to the Tonic as in a Major or minor tonality). One characteristic pattern is the wide leaps of the rising fifth followed by a rise to the octave. The Free Rhythm (unmetered) is free flowing and unmeasured.

Go to **GSGMUSIC.com** - Free Resources - listen to **Ordo Virtutum** Scene 4. Answer the Questions below.

1. Circle if the Ordo Virtutum Scene 4 begins with the Devil: singing *cantible* or (speaking *strepitus.*)

2. Circle if the Ordo Vitutum sung by the Soul (Anima) is in: (monophonic texture) or homophonic texture.

3. Circle if the Ordo Virtutum melodic motive is based on: Major scales or (modes) or minor scales.

4. Circle if the rhythmic meter of the Ordo Vitutum is: (unmetered) or duple meter or triple meter.

5. Circle if the Performing Forces of the Ordo Vitutum are: solo voices or chorus or (both.)

6. Circle if the Genre of the Ordo Vitutum is: opera or (morality play) or ballet.

7. Circle if the Ordo Vitutum modal melody is: (plainchant) or contrapuntal or minor modality.

MUSIC HISTORY - 13th CENTURY- SUMMER IS ICUMEN IN

In the early **Medieval Era**, sacred (religious) works were in monophonic texture (one melodic line). In the later Middle Ages, secular (non religious) works emerged in polyphonic texture (more than one melodic line).

The first polyphonic form, known as *organum* (an extra vocal part of parallel fourths or fifths), gave Medieval polyphony its unique sound. Later, *organum* incorporated 3 and 4 voices that led to polyphonic imitation (repetition of a melody at a different pitch level in a different voice) called contrapuntal or polyphonic texture.

In the 13th Century, composers discovered how to use imitation with two or more voices chasing each other. *Caccia* (chase or hunt) is a technique called Canon, when voices (or instrumental parts) sing or play the same music starting at different times (chasing each other). Exact imitation is called a Canon.

A Round is a simple type of Canon. In a Round, each voice, when finished, can start again at the beginning so the piece goes "round and round" (such as "Row, Row, Row your Boat").

The English poem **"Sumer Is Icumen In"** (or Cuckoo Song - c.1250), sung in the form of a *Rota* (Medieval term for Round) is a joyous celebration of the coming of summer as the cuckoo song heralds rejuvenation.

Sumer Is Icumen In (Modern English - Summer Is Come) is in imitative polyphonic texture. Genre: Perpetual Round (a vocal work in the form of an imitative round). Performing Forces: Six voices *a cappella* (unaccompanied).

Sumer Is Icumen In is written in square notated polyphony on a five-line staff for six voices. This catchy lilting melody is sung in Middle English with syllabic text setting (each syllable of a word is broken up and assigned to an individual note). Form: *Rota* - Sung 3 times over 2-voice bass ostinato.

Lower voices: A 4-measure melody is sung by basses in a two-voice round. Repetition of the round creates an *ostinato* (repeated musical pattern).

Upper voices: Four-voice round sing the simple rhythmic pattern of long-short-long-short in the melody in imitation as the bass *ostinato* pattern continues creating a modern harmonic sound of 3rds and 6ths.

Sumer Is Icumen In (anonymous) was written for 6 voices and may be sung in Middle English *"Sumer Is Icumen In"* or in Modern English *"Summer is a-coming in"*. The melody is organized as a canon. The bass part has its own 4-measure phrase, used as a round, with its repetition serving as a bass ostinato to the round of the upper voices. This piece can be performed by one or more voices/instruments.

Go to **GSGMUSIC.com** - Easy Access to videos of various performances of *Sumer Is Icumen In.*

1. *Sumer Is Icumen In* was written in the __13ᵗʰ__ Century in the Period called the __Medieval__ Era.

2. The Composer of *Sumer Is Icumen In* is simply identified as __anonymous__

3. The Genre of *Sumer Is Icumen In* is __Perpetual Round__

4. The Performing Forces of *Sumer Is Icumen In* is __Six voices a cappella__

5. *Sumer Is Icumen In* is in the form of a *Rota*, meaning __Medieval term for Round__

6. *Sumer Is Icumen In* in Modern English is __Summer is a-coming in__

7. Simple type of Canon where each voice starts again at the beginning is called a __Round__

MUSIC HISTORY - SUMMER IS ICUMEN IN - READING ROTA

Sumer Is Icumen In (also called the Summer Canon or the Cuckoo Song or the Reading Rota) is written in the form of a *rota* (round). An opening four measure ostinato in the bass is followed by four tenor voices, each part entering one at a time creating a round. This happy dancelike English melody celebrates renewal.

Sumer Is Icumen In is called **"Reading Rota"** because the manuscript was found at Reading Abbey (one of the wealthiest and most important monasteries of medieval England), and *rota* is the old name for a round. The unknown composer may have been a monk in Reading Abbey or copied from an earlier manuscript.

Go to **GSGMUSIC.com** - Free Resources - Listen to *Sumer Is Icumen In*. Answer the Questions below.

1. Circle if *Sumer Is Icumen In* begins with the: (lower voice) or upper voice.

2. Circle if *Sumer Is Icumen In* is in: monophonic texture or homophonic texture or (polyphonic texture).

3. Circle if *Sumer Is Icumen In* is based on: (a poem) or a variation of another piece or a story.

4. Circle if the two-voice bass pattern is: a long-short-long-short pattern or (an ostinato of a musical idea).

5. Circle if the four-voice tenor pattern is in the form of a: (canon) or chorus or solo.

6. Circle if the Genre of *Sumer Is Icumen In* is: opera or morality play or (perpetual round).

7. Circle if *Sumer Is Icumen In* is also called: The Cricket or (Reading Rota) or Ordo Vitutum.

MUSIC HISTORY - RENAISSANCE ERA (*ca* 1450 - *ca* 1600) - JOSQUIN DES PREZ

Renaissance Era (French: *Rebirth*), the period between Medieval (500 - 1450) and Baroque (1600 - 1750), was a period of revival, discoveries and new beginnings. One of the great masters of contrapuntal style was **Josquin des Pres**, who composed both sacred (***Ave Maria … virgo serena*** - *motet,* unaccompanied sacred choral work*)* and secular (***El grillo*** - *frottola,* light and playful secular work), polyphonic works.

The Franco-Flemish master composer Josquin des Prez (*ca* 1440-1521) is one of the most musically ingenious and highly admired Renaissance composers.

Josquin learned music by singing in a church choir, becoming a member of the Pope's choir in Rome and eventually a court composer to King Louis XII of France. Much of Josquin's music was written as sacred church music.

Josquin also wrote secular *chansons* (light charming songs) that moved along in chords (harmonic sections). He has been called the "father of modern harmony."

Josquin des Prez was a good-humored man who often wrote little musical jokes in his works (once even in a motet to embarrass Louis XII, who forgot to give him a promised gift). Josquin's humor is evident in his composition *El grillo* (The Cricket) which evokes word painting in the playful poem written as a tuneful song.

El grillo (The Cricket), based on the poem by Jean Molinetand, is one of Josquin's most popular *frottola*.

Genre: *Frottola* - a type of popular Italian secular polyphonic vocal work, usually written for four voice parts based on a comic or playful poem using word painting.

Word Painting (Tone Painting or Text Painting) is the technique of writing music using melody, harmony and/or rhythm to reflect the meaning of the words in the song. The word painting (connection of the music to the text) of the poem brings this delightful song to life as a four part *frottola* about the cricket.

Josquin uses homorhythmic texture (same rhythmic pattern) for all voices in blocked chordal style (chord built directly below the melody).

Performing Forces: Four voices. Josquin's masterful lighthearted expression is evident in the *a cappella* (unaccompanied) *El grillo.*

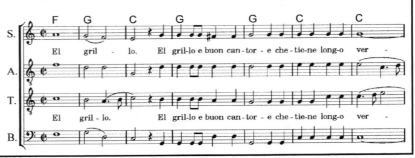

Go to **GSGMUSIC.com** - For Easy Access to listening to Josquin des Prez "*El grillo*" (The Cricket) *Frottola.*

1. Josquin des Prez is one of the most admired composers of the <u>Renaissance</u> Era.

2. The Era (*ca* 1450 - 1600) between the Medieval and Baroque Period was French for <u>Rebirth</u>.

3. Josquin wrote both <u>Sacred</u> music for church and <u>secular</u> music for chansons.

4. Josquin's *El grillo* means: The <u>Cricket</u> and is written in the Genre: <u>Frottola</u>.

5. The technique of connecting the music to the text is called <u>Word Painting</u>.

6. The same rhythmic pattern used for all voices in *El grillo* is called <u>homorhythmic</u> texture.

7. Chords built directly below the melody create a <u>blocked chordal</u> style.

MUSIC HISTORY - JOSQUIN DES PREZ - EL GRILLO

Josquin des Prez - *El grillo* (The Cricket) is a Madrigal - music which closely follows the rhythm & meaning of a short poem. Word Painting, the emotional feeling of the poem, is mirrored in the melody and harmony of the music. *El grillo* mirrors the "longo verso" (cricket's long notes) and "dalle beve" (cricket's short notes).

A Madrigal was a Renaissance secular work for voices, set to a short, lyric poem. A Madrigal is a four part *a cappella* vocal piece sung for entertainment. Sections may be homorhythmic (all voices sing the same rhythm) while other sections may be contrapuntal (polyphonic texture - imitation between voices in this song) as in "dalle beve". Light tuneful madrigals were called *frottola* (popular song) or *chansons* in France.

Josquin des Prez - *El grillo* (The Cricket) Lyrics   (Note: There are various English translations.)

	Original Italian Text	English Translation
Section 1	El grillo è buon cantore,	(The cricket is a good singer,)
	Che tienne longo verso,	(And he sings for a long time,)
	Dalle beve grillo canta.	(Give him a drink so he can go on singing.)
Section 2	Ma non fa come gli altri uccelli,	(But he doesn't do what the other birds do,)
	Come li han cantato un poco,	(Who after singing a little,)
	Van' de fatto in altro loco.	(Just go elsewhere.)
	Sempre el grillo sta pur saldo,	(The cricket is always steadfast,)
Section 3	Quando la maggior è'l caldo,	(When it is hottest,)
	Al' hor canta sol per amore.	(Then he sings just for love.)

Word Painting in *El grillo* is used in the length of the cricket's 'longo verso', symbolized by long notes (*longas*) with a *fermata* in the two outer voices.

Polyphonic texture is used in imitation style of the 'dalle beve', symbolized by short notes in echo-like cricket sounds.

The 'longo verso' and 'dalle beve' contrast the rhythm of long and short.

La Festa del Grillo was a feast (folklorist event) that took place in Florence, Italy in the Renaissance Era. The cricket, a symbol of the arrival of spring, was also a danger to harvest. Crickets were captured and put into elegant little boxes. At the Festa del Grillo, young men would give them to their beloved ladies as a gift.

Go to **GSGMUSIC.com** - Free Resources - Listen to *El grillo* (The Cricket). Answer the Questions below.

1. Circle if *El grillo* begins with the: 'dalle beve' (short notes) or ('longo verso' (long notes)).

2. Circle if *El grillo* opening 4-voice chordal style is in: (homorhythmic texture) or polyrhythmic texture.

3. Circle if *El grillo* is based on: (a poem) or a variation of another piece or a story.

4. Circle if *El grillo* "dalle beve" section is in: homophonic texture or (polyphonic texture.)

5. Circle if *El grillo* uses word painting to express the: 'longo verso' or 'dalle beve' or (both.)

6. Circle if the Genre of *El grillo* is: (frottola) or morality play or perpetual round.

7. Circle if *El grillo* is also called: (The Cricket) or Reading Rota or Ordo Vitutum.

MUSIC HISTORY - GLOBAL MUSIC STYLES - JAVANESE GAMELAN

Global Music (also called World Music or International Music) encompasses different styles of music from around the globe. Non-European music includes many forms of folk and tribal music of the Middle East, Africa, Asia, Central and South America, and Indonesian music.

One form of Global Music is Gamelan, with two principal styles: Balinese Gamelan and Javanese Gamelan. The Javanese Gamelan is the traditional music of Java, an island in Southeast Asia.

 Java is one of the thousands of islands of Indonesia which stretches across almost 3,400 miles of ocean. Java, the most populated island in Indonesia, has more than half the population of Indonesia (over 260 million) living there.

Java has rich well-known Indonesian music culture called Gamelan. A traditional ensemble of Gamelan consists of tuned and untuned instruments (primarily percussion) using metallophones, gongs, drums, wooden xylophones, plus bamboo flutes, bowed & plucked strings and voices.

Gamelan (Javanese word "gamel" meaning to strike or hammer) is a traditional Javanese instrumental ensemble of mostly percussion instruments. Javanese gamelan (although notated), is primarily taught through the oral tradition of much time spent listening, imitating and observing gamelan performances.

Metallophones are tuned percussion instruments with different sized tuned metal bars struck with mallets creating a bell-like sound used in Gamelan. These are tuned to a distinctive scale pattern.

There are two Gamelan tunings: the sléndro (five-note scale) and the pélog (seven-note scale). Javanese gamelan music (traditionally associated with royalty) is calm and regal with cycles of various shifting tempos, lively repeated (ostinato) melodies, driving (motoric) rhythms and extended improvisation.

 Cirebon, founded in 1369 on the north coast of the island of Java, was the royal city of the ancient Javanese kingdom. Cirebon had an important influence in the development of Javanese art - including Gamelan.

One of the five classical Cirebon genres is *gamelan prawa*, a form of "gamelan proper", presented in the Javanese Gamelan - *Kaboran (Gamelan Prawa)* - Gamelan of Java, Vol 5; Cirebon Tradition in America.

Go to **GSGMUSIC.com** - Free Resources - Easy access to LEVEL 8 - Watch the videos to learn more about the music of the Javanese Gamelan. Listen to *Kaboran (Gamelan Prawa)*. Answer the questions below.

1. World Music or International Music from around the globe is called _Global Music_.

2. One form of traditional world music of Java is called Javanese _Gamelan_.

3. The Javanese word "gamel" means to _strike hammer_ the percussion instruments in the ensemble.

4. The two Gamelan tunings are called _sléndro (5 note scale)_ and _pélog (7 note scale)_.

5. The ancient Javanese kingdom's royal city of _Cirebon_ was an important influence of Gamelan.

6. A traditional ensemble of Gamelan uses primarily _tuned percussion_ instruments.

7. Percussion instruments with different sized tuned metal bars stuck by mallets are _metallophones_.

MUSIC HISTORY - JAVANESE GAMELAN - KABORAN (GAMELAN PRAWA)

Javanese Gamelan "Kaboran (Gamelan Prawa)" - *Kaboran* is a classical overture piece played (for the entertainment of the spirits and enjoyment of the gamelan musicians) at the elaborate all night *Wayang Kulit* (long complex dramas) shadow puppet show theater in Cirebon.

Wayang refers to the puppet theater. *Kulit* means skin and refers to the leather construction of the puppets that are carefully chiseled with very fine tools and operated with shaped handles and rods controlled by the puppeteer. The puppeteer (dalang) sits behind a screen (kelir) as the puppet figures are rear-projected with a coconut-oil (or electric) light on to a linen screen made of white cotton stretched on a wooden frame.

Gamelan Prawa instruments, using the sléndro (five-note scale pattern) tuning, include metallaphones and gongs. Various sizes of of gongs and metallophones create multiple pitch layers. The layered texture is one characteristic: the music of low pitched instruments moves slowly and high pitched instruments, fast.

Metallophones & Gongs

Ageng - Largest of the hanging gongs.
Suwukan - Mid-size hanging gongs.
Kempul - Smallest hanging gongs.

Kenong - Largest of the horizontal gongs resting on racks.
Kethuk and *Kempyang* - Two small horizontal gongs which form a pair.

The Global Music of Javanese Gamelan had an eye-opening impact on many musicians, including French Impressionist composer Claude Debussy. Debussy (1862- 1918) born in St. Germain-en-Laye, a suburb of Paris, first heard Gamelan music in 1889 at the Paris Universal Exposition (World's Fair for which the Eiffel Tower was built). He spent many hours at the Java exhibit listening to the complexities of the Gamelan.

Debussy's pieces written after 1890 contained gamelan-like layered texture. Debussy used the pentatonic (5-note) scale with the 5-note sléndro tuning of the Javanese to imitate the sound of the gamelan on the piano in his composition *Pagodes* (from *Estampes*).

"Do you remember the Javanese music, able to express every shade of meaning, even unmentionable shades . . . which make our tonic and dominant seem like ghosts..."
~ Claude Debussy

Go to **GSGMUSIC.com** - Easy access to Listen to *Kaboran* and *Pagodes*. Check the correct answers below.

Javanese "Kaboran" is a classical overture piece played by the:

☑ Gamelan Ensemble   ☐ Symphony Orchestra

Gamelan percussion instruments with tuned metal bars played with mallets are called:

☐ bamboo flutes   ☑ metallophones

A traditional Javanese instrumental ensemble consisting of various tuned and untuned instruments is:

☑ gamelan   ☐ wayang

Dubussy's *Pagodes* (from *Estampes*) for the piano was based on the Javanese scale tuning:

☐ pélog   ☑ sléndro

MUSIC HISTORY - THE RAGA IN INDIAN CLASSICAL MUSIC

Global Music - **Indian Classical Music**, one of the oldest forms of music, was passed down in oral tradition. Melodically and rhythmically, the complexity of Indian music was emulated by 20th century composers such as: Stravinsky (The Rite of Spring), Messiaen (Symphony Turangalîla, originally called 'tâlas') and Bartók.

The Four Main Elements of Indian Classical Music are: Drone, Melody, Rhythm and Improvisation.

Drone: Two notes act as a foundation (atonal center), as it does not have harmony as in Western music.
Melody: Melodic structure of Indian *raga* is based on a pattern of pitches on which the melody is improvised.
Rhythm: Added gradually, a basic rhythmic cycle of *tala* is repeated in many complex rhythmic patterns.
Improvisation: As music is not notated, musicians improvise within a set of rules based on the *raga* and *tala*.

In the music (*raga*), the simplicity of the drone is contrasted by the complexity of the rhythmic structure (*tala*).

The *Raga* is played by melody instruments, the most popular is the *Sitar*.
The *Tala* is played by percussion instruments, the most popular is the *Tabla*.

Sitar - a multi-stringed plucked instrument with moveable metal frets. The Sitar has a distinctive timbre and resonance from sympathetic strings, uniquely shaped bridge, long hollow neck and a gourd-shaped resonance chamber creating melody, drone and percussive effects.

Tabla - consists of two single headed, barrel shaped small drums of slightly different size and shape. The playing technique is complex and involves extensive use of the fingers and palms in various configurations to create a variety of different sounds and rhythms.

Stringed instruments, such as the *sitar*, play melodically while syncopated cross-rhythms are played on the *tabla*.
Raga forms the melodic structure while *Tala* forms the rhythmic cycle.

Raga - meaning 'color, passion or emotion', is having the ability to 'color the mind' to affect the emotions or atmosphere of the listener. A melodic structure of notes based on a pattern of pitches and intervals (tones and microtones - smaller than a half step) serve as the basis for melodic improvisation. *Raga* and *Tala* are open frameworks for creativity and an infinite number of possibilities.

Tala - meaning 'clap', is the musical meter. The *Tala* forms the metrical structure that repeats in a rhythmic cycle, from the beginning to end of the music. The *Tala* is not restricted to rhythmic pulses of "strong, weak" beats, but is flexible as the accent of a beat is decided by the shape of the musical phrase. A metric cycle (repeated rhythmic structure) of a *Tala* contains a specific number of beats (3 beats to 128 beats).

Go to **GSGMUSIC.com** - Free Resources For Easy Access to listening to Raga Indian Classical Music.

1. 4 Main Elements of Indian Classical Music are: <u>Drone, Melody, Rhythm, Improvisation</u>.

2. Indian Classical Music, one of the oldest forms of music, was taught by <u>oral tradition</u>.

3. The extended improvised Indian Classical Music performance meaning 'color' is called <u>Raga</u>.

4. The most popular multi-stringed plucked instrument used in Indian Classical Music is the <u>Sitar</u>.

5. Musical meter ('clap') that forms the metrical structure of a repeated rhythmic cycle is <u>Tala</u>.

6. The most popular drum percussion instrument used in Indian Classical Music is the <u>Tabla</u>.

7. The two note atonal center that acts as a foundation in Indian Classical Music is called <u>Drone</u>.

MUSIC HISTORY - RAGA IN INDIAN CLASSICAL MUSIC - "EVENING RAGA: BHOPALI"

Modern influence of Raga in Indian Music is known in the western world through the work of Grammy Award Winning Indian *sitar* musician **Ravi Shankar** (1920 - 2012), known as the **"godfather of world music."** His famous daughters, Norah Jones and Anoushka Shankar, released "Traces of You" shortly after his death.

George Harrison (guitarist from The Beatles) took *sitar* lessons from Ravi Shankar in the 1960's. Harrison played the *sitar* on The Beatles hits "Norwegian Wood (This Bird Has Flown)" and "Within You Without You".

Ragas in Indian Music represent their own "color" which can affect the mood of the listener. Different *ragas* are played at different times of the day: morning, afternoon, evening and night, each expressing a mood of happiness, courage, humor, peace, etc. Musicians may choose the *raga* based on their mood at the time, as in **Irshad Khan's "Evening Raga: *Bhopali*"** from The Magic of Twilight.

Irshad Khan, a child prodigy, is internationally recognized as one of the world's leading players of the *Sitar* and *Surbahar* (bass sitar - invented by his great great grandfather Ustad Sahebdad Khan). An exponent of the teachings of Indian Classical Music, Irshad Khan is the founder of the Universal Academy for Musicians in Mississauga, Ontario, Canada and Mumbai (Bombay), India and Rochester, New York.

"I am connected to both my instruments - sitar and surbahar, but I have different emotional attachments to each.

I express my mood and feelings through my instruments and converse with them differently. Playing the sitar is a deeply spiritual and romantic experience while playing the surbahar is deeply spiritual and devotional." ~ Irshad Khan

Photo Credit: Used with permission from Irshad Khan.

Khan's "Evening Raga: *Bhopali*" from The Magic of Twilight (22:25 min) is a classical *raga* based on a pentatonic scale and evokes a musical conversation through improvisation. The basic *tala* or rhythmic cycle begins slowly and gradually increases in speed. Performing Forces: Sitar, Tabla and Tanpoora.

The Tanpoora (tambura or tanpura) is a long-necked plucked string instrument. The repeated plucking of a cycle of four strings in a continuous loop provides a continuous harmonic drone and supports the melody.

Go to **GSGMUSIC.com** - Free Resources - Easy access to watch Irshad Khan's performance on the sitar.

1. Listen to the music of "Evening Raga: *Bhopali*" The Magic of Twilight. Check (✓) the correct answer.

The Indian *sitar* musician performing the "Raga: *Bhopali*" from The Magic of Twilight is:

[✓] Irshad Khan   [ ] Ravi Shankar   [ ] Ustad Sahebdad Khan

The color or mood indicated in the Raga: *Bhopali* The Magic of Twilight represents the time of day as:

[ ] morning   [ ] afternoon   [✓] evening

The *Tala* of the Raga: *Bhopali* is the rhythmic cycle that progresses from:

[ ] fast to slow   [ ] fast to slow to fast   [✓] slow to fast

---

The Sitar, Tabla and Tanpoora create a mood through improvisation of Raga: *Bhopali* that evokes a:

[✓] musical conversation   [ ] morning frustration   [ ] violent argument

---

MUSIC HISTORY - OVERVIEW MEDIEVAL, RENAISSANCE, BAROQUE and CLASSICAL ERAS

Music History through the ages has evolved in both sacred and secular music. The elements of music in melody, harmony, rhythm, dynamics, texture, phrasing and voicing continue to develop creating new sounds.

Review Music History in the UMT Supplemental Workbooks LEVELS 1 - 8.
Use the Style & Characteristics word bank to fill in the chart below. Not all words will be used.

Medieval - Renaissance (ca 476 - 1450 - 1600) (Style & Characteristics)	Baroque (1600 - 1750) (Style & Characteristics)	Classical (1750 - 1825) (Style & Characteristics)
✓Monophonic Canon ✓Polyphonic ✓Free Rhythm ✓Plainchant ✓Homorhythmic ✓Perpetual Round ✓Word Painting Madrigal ✓Ostinato ✓Rota ✓Frottola	✓Invention Mordent ✓Concerto Grosso ✓Motive ✓Sequence ✓Oratorio ✓Augmentation ✓Chorus Inversion ✓Ritornello Form ✓Countermotive ✓Transposition	✓Rondo Form ✓Coloratura Soprano ✓Aria The Magic Flute ✓Opera ✓Chamber Music ✓Homophonic ✓Sonata Form ✓Concerto ✓Rocket Theme ✓Theme and Variation Symphony
Plainchant a modal melody, in Latin text, Medieval Era	**Chorus** large group of singers, voice parts SATB	**Sonata Form** Exposition, Development, Recapitulation.
Free Rhythm is flowing rhythm, (unmetered), unmeasured	**Motive** short musical idea that develops a theme	**Coloratura Soprano** highly agile, trained voice, *Queen of the Night*
Perpetual Round imitative canon, *Sumer Is Icumen In*	**Ritornello Form** shifts between *ripieno* and *concertino*	**Theme + Variation** theme played, repeated with changes
Monophonic Texture single melodic line, *Ordo Vitutum*	**Augmentation** rhythmic note value increased (often doubled)	**Opera** a musical drama with singing and costumes
Rota name for a Medieval round in canon style	**Invention** contrapuntal piece, equal multi-voice texture	**Rondo Form** 3 alternating principle themes A, B and C
Homorhythmic Texture, all voices same rhythmic pattern	**Sequence** repetition of motive at higher or lower pitches	**Concerto** solo(ists) instrumental 'against' orchestra
Polyphonic Texture multi voice singing, *Reading Rota*	**Oratorio** production of religious story, music & song	**Homophonic** Texture single voice, harmonic accomp.
Ostinato repeated rhythmic or melodic pattern	**Countermotive** different motive appears against motive	**Rocket Theme** opening tutti, motive - *Eine kleine Nachtmusik*
Frottola secular polyphonic vocal based on poem	**Concerto Grosso** solo (group), accompanied by instrumental group	**Chamber Music** genre of small string ensemble, (entertain)
Word Painting music that mirrors the words, *El grillo*	**Transposition** repetition of motive, same voice, different pitch	**Aria** lyric song for solo voice & orchestra, emotional

MUSIC HISTORY - OVERVIEW ROMANTIC and MODERN ERAS, and GLOBAL MUSIC STYLES

Music History continues to be written using new styles of electronic music and electronic instruments. The influences of Global Music fused into the modern genres produce the unique musical sounds of tomorrow.

Review Music History in the UMT Supplemental Workbooks LEVELS 1 - 8.
Use the Style & Characteristics word bank to fill in the chart below. Not all words will be used.

Romantic (1825 - 1900)	Modern (1900 - present)	Global (World Music)
(Style & Characteristics)	(Style & Characteristics)	(Style & Characteristics)
✓Program Music ✓Concert Overture ✓Nationalism Ternary Form ✓Chromatic Harmony ✓Symphonic Poem ✓Ballet Poet of the Piano ✓Romanticism ✓Virtuoso ✓Rubato ✓Étude	✓Musique concrète ✓Celesta ✓Polytonality Amplitude ✓Jazz ✓Petrushka Chord ✓Verse-Chorus Structure ✓Electronic Music ✓Sackbut ✓Dripsody Pentatonic Scale ✓12-Bar Blues	✓Gamelan ✓Metallophones ✓Raga ✓Tala ✓Sitar ✓Tabla Surbahar ✓Drone ✓Improvisation ✓Sléndro Pélog ✓Gamelan Prawa
Virtuoso highly skilled performer, often composer	**Polytonality** 2 + keys simultaneously create dissonance	**Sitar** plucked multi-stringed Indian instrument
Nationalism music ideas showcase composer's patriotism	**Verse-Chorus Structure** genre of *Over the Rainbow - Wizard of Oz*	**Gamelan** Javanese instrumental ensemble of Java
Romanticism emotionally expressive, imaginative work	**Electronic Music** produced through devices, tape recorders	**Tala** repeated rhythmic cycle, meter used in Raga
Concert Overture single mvt. concert piece for orchestra	**Jazz** syncopation swing rhythm pulse, improvisation	**Improvisation** music not notated, musicians "make up"
Étude French for study, techniques for dexterity	**Dripsody** manipulated sound of water drop, electronically	**Raga** colorful Indian melodic improvisation
Ballet non-verbal story told through music & dance	**12 Bar Blues** Progression of chords 3 four-measure phrases	**Sléndro** 5-note scale pattern pentatonic gamelan tuning
Symphonic Poem single mvt. free form orchestral program work	**Music Concrète** electronic experimental music (diff sounds)	**Drone** sustained sound of tone(s) atonal foundation
Rubato flexible tempo, "robbed time"	**Petruska chord** polychord of C Major & F♯ Major (tritone apart)	**Tabla** two single headed barrel shaped small drums
Program Music descriptive title, literary or pictorial program	**Sackbut** first voltage controlled synthesizer & keyboard	**Metallophones** tuned percussion instruments & mallets
Chromatic harmony dissonance, notes not belonging to the key	**Celesta** keyboard percussion instrument, bell sound	**Gamelan Prawa** Cirebon genre of *Kaboran* (Javanese)

MUSIC HISTORY - MUSICAL ERAS REVIEW

Music History in the UMT Supplemental Workbook Series (PREP LEVEL and LEVELS 1 - 8).

PREP LEVEL: Medieval Period (around 500 - 1450), Renaissance Period (1450 - 1600), Baroque Period (1600 - 1750), Classical Period (1750 to 1825), Romantic Period (1825 - 1900) & 20th/21st Century Period.

LEVEL 1: Orchestral Instruments, Story Telling Through Sound, Prokofiev (Peter and the Wolf) and Camille Saint-Saëns (Carnival of the Animals).

LEVEL 2: Symphony & Opera, Mozart (Twelve Variations on Ah, Vous Dirai-Je Maman), Concerto, Rondo Form, (Horn Concerto No. 4 in E flat Major).

LEVEL 3: Bach, (Anna Magdalena Notebook), Baroque Dances, Petzod (Menuet in G Major), J.S. Bach (French Suite No. 5 in G Major - Gavotte and Gigue).

LEVEL 4: Orchestra Families & Instruments, Britten (Young Person's Guide to the Orchestra), Tchaikovsky (The Nutcracker - Sugar Plum Fairy and Waltz of the Flowers).

LEVEL 5: Voices in Vocal Music, Relationship between Music & Text, Handel (Hallelujah Chorus from Messiah), Mozart (Queen of the Night - The Magic Flute), Arlen (Over the Rainbow).

LEVEL 6: J.S. Bach (Invention in C Major No. 1), Brandenburg Concertos (Concerto No. 5 First Movement) and Mozart (Eine Kleine Nachtmusik).

LEVEL 7: Mendelssohn (Overture to A Midsummer Night's Dream), Chopin (Etude in C Minor, Op. 10 No. 12 Revolutionary), Stravinsky (Petrushka), Le Caine (Dripsody) and Ellington (Ko-Ko).

LEVEL 8: Hildegard von Bingen, Josquin des Prez, Irshad Khan and works of annon. composers.

Go to **GSGMUSIC.com** - Free Resources for Videos to review Music History. Answer the questions below.

1. Instruments produce their own unique tone color that defines their sound called _timbre_.

2. The orchestral stringed instrument with the lowest pitch in the string family is the _Bass_.

3. Keyboard instrument with quills to pluck the strings is called the _Harpsichord_.

4. Bach's Allemande, Menuet, Gavotte, Gigue and Bourrée are known as _Baroque_ Dances.

5. The piano made it possible to play _melody_ and _harmony_ together.

6. The Young Person's Guide to the Orchestra was written by British composer _Benjamin Britten_.

7. Rustics "Bottom" comical character from Mendelssohn's Concert Overture turned into a _Donkey_.

8. Mendelssohn's Concert Overture is based on Shakespeare's play _A Midsummer Night's Dream_.

MUSIC HISTORY - COMPOSERS and THEIR FAMOUS WORKS REVIEW

Composers may compose in various genres or identify with one genre. Their works reflect their own unique style of composition. By studying music history, composers and their works, we learn how their life, style, instruments available to them and the period they lived in is reflected and expressed through their music.

Go to **GSGMUSIC.com** - Free Resources - Listen to Various Genres of Music. Analyze the Rhythm, Meter, Melody, Harmony, Dynamics, Timbre, Texture, Vocal Ranges and Instruments that create each unique work.

1. Complete the Music History Review Chart below.

Ordo Virtutum Composer: _Hildegard von Bingen_ Period: _Medieval Era (ca. 476-1450)_

Genre: _Morality Play_ Texture: _monophonic_

Plainchant means: _modal melody in free rhythm (monophonic)_.

Performing Forces: _17 Female Voices / 1 Male Voice_ Also called "Play of _Virtues_".

Sumer Is Icumen In Composer: _anonymous_ Period: _13th Century (medieval Era)_

Genre: _Perpetual Round_ Texture: _polyphonic_

English text of title means: _Summer is Come_ Ostinato means: _repeated pattern (melodic/rhythmic)_

Performing Forces: _Six Voices a cappella_ Rota means: _Round_

El grillo Composer: _Josquin des Prez_ Period: _Renaissance (ca. 1450-1600)_

Genre: _Frottola_ Texture: _homorhythmic and polyphonic_

English Text of title means: _The Cricket_ A cappella means: _without accompaniment_

Performing Forces: _4 voices_ Word Painting means: _text is mirrored in music_

Kaboran (Gamelan Prawa) Type of music known as: _Javanese Gamelan_

Metallophones are struck with _mallets_. World Music Style also called _Global_ Music.

Kaboran is performed for the: _Overture piece of (Wayang Kulit) Shadow Puppet Show_

Performing Forces: _Gamelan Javanese instrumental ensemble_

Bhopali - The Magic of Twilight - Type: _Evening Raga_ Style: _Classical Raga_

Raga means: _'color the mind'_ Tala means: _'clap' (musical meter)_

The time of day this musical conversation would be performed is _evening_.

Performing Forces: _Sitar, Tabla, Tanpoora_

MUSIC HISTORY - THE INFLUENCE OF GLOBAL MUSIC

Global Music and Award Winning Indian *sitar* musician **Ravi Shankar**, the "Godfather of world music", had a powerful influence on many musicians and composers including: The Beatles guitarist George Harrison, violinist Yehudi Menuhin, minimalist composer Philip Glass and Jazz Legend guitarist **Lenny Breau**.

Lenny Breau (1941 - 1984), an American-born Juno Award winning guitarist, was one of the most admired guitarist of his generation.

He was known for blending many styles of music including jazz, country, classical, flamenco and Indian music.

Breau, influenced by the emotional sound of Ravi Shankar's *sitar*, purchased his first *sitar*. After intense practicing, he performed on a 1967 CBC TV session, but he was no threat to Ravi Shakar.

Breau strummed modal sounding melodic fragments on the principal and sympathetic strings of the *sitar* over top of his own twelve-string guitar work creating an interesting melting pot of sound. During the 60's Indian modal phrases could be heard in his free form style. Breau was known for his harmonic playing.

Lenny Breau was inspired by guitarist Chet Atkins, known as "Mr. Guitar". Breau used staggering finger style techniques not often used in jazz guitar. By using a seven-string guitar and approaching the guitar like a piano, his evocative effortless style opened up possibilities for the innovation of the instrument.

Lenny Breau toured extensively with his parents Hal Lone Pine and Betty Cody along with his brother in law, **Ray St. Germain**.

Ray St. Germain, Award Winning Entertainer and Canadian Country Music Hall of Fame Inductee, performed with Breau on the road, and on the CBC National TV Show (Winnipeg) "Music Hop Hootenanny", hosted by Ray.

Go to **GSGMUSIC.com** - Free Resources LEVEL 8 to watch videos and learn more about Music History.

1. Answer the following questions on the influence of Global Music. Check (✓) the correct answer below.

Ravi Shankar influenced many composers and musicians such as:		
☑ George Harrison	☐ Duke Ellington	☐ Hugh Le Caine

Playing the *sitar* was explored by many professional musicians including:		
☐ Chet Atkins	☑ Lenny Breau	☐ Ray St. Germain

Lenny Breau played a seven-string guitar and approached the guitar like a:		
☐ *sitar*	☐ violin	☑ piano

The influence of Global Music is apparent by *sitar* musician Ravi Shankar known as:		
☐ Mr. Guitar	☐ Jazz Legend	☑ Godfather of world music

Music Maestro - Name the Composer

So-La Says: Write the composers name below each composition title.

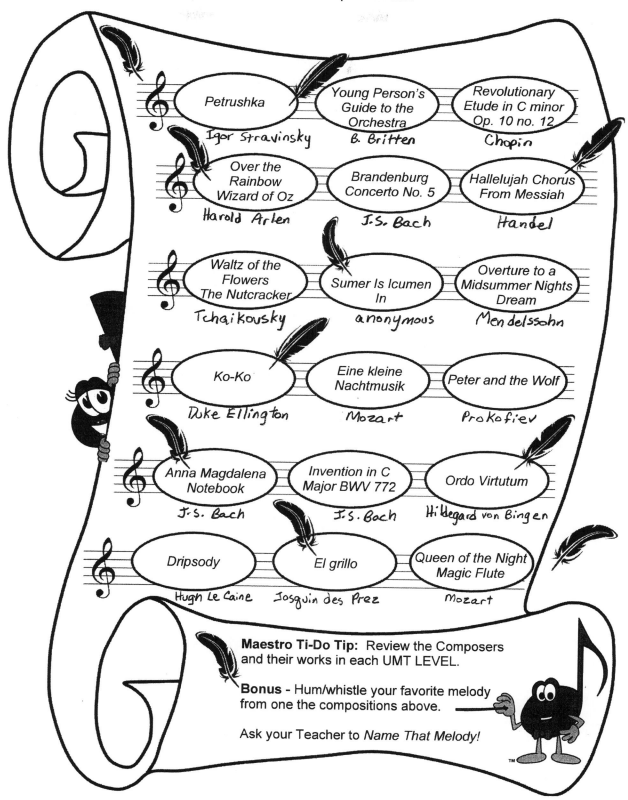

Petrushka	Young Person's Guide to the Orchestra	Revolutionary Etude in C minor Op. 10 no. 12
Igor Stravinsky	B. Britten	Chopin

Over the Rainbow Wizard of Oz	Brandenburg Concerto No. 5	Hallelujah Chorus From Messiah
Harold Arlen	J.S. Bach	Handel

Waltz of the Flowers The Nutcracker	Sumer Is Icumen In	Overture to a Midsummer Nights Dream
Tchaikovsky	anonymous	Mendelssohn

Ko-Ko	Eine kleine Nachtmusik	Peter and the Wolf
Duke Ellington	Mozart	Prokofiev

Anna Magdalena Notebook	Invention in C Major BWV 772	Ordo Virtutum
J.S. Bach	J.S. Bach	Hildegard von Bingen

Dripsody	El grillo	Queen of the Night Magic Flute
Hugh Le Caine	Josquin des Prez	Mozart

Maestro Ti-Do Tip: Review the Composers and their works in each UMT LEVEL.

Bonus - Hum/whistle your favorite melody from one the compositions above.

Ask your Teacher to *Name That Melody!*

Ultimate Music Theory
Level 8 Theory Exam

Total Score: _____
100

The Ultimate Music Theory™ Rudiments Workbooks, Supplemental Workbooks and Exams prepare students for successful completion of the Royal Conservatory of Music Theory Levels.

1. a) Write the following intervals above each of the given notes.

10

      dim 11   Maj 6   Aug 9   Per 5   min 10

b) Invert the above intervals in the Treble Clef. Name the inversions.

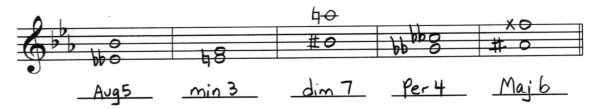

    Aug5   min 3   dim 7   Per 4   Maj 6

c) Name the following intervals.

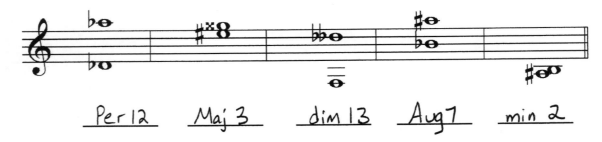

    Per 12   Maj 3   dim 13   Aug 7   min 2

d) Invert the above intervals in the Bass Clef. Name the inversions.

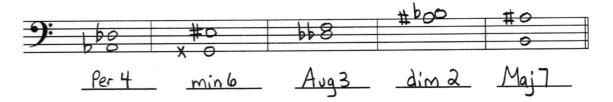

    Per 4   min 6   Aug 3   dim 2   Maj 7

2. a) Write the following chords in the Treble Clef. Use a Key Signature and any necessary accidentals. Use whole notes. Write the Root/Quality and the Functional Chord Symbols for each.

10

- i) The Dominant Seventh Chord of b flat minor, in first inversion.
- ii) The Mediant Triad of c sharp minor, harmonic form, in second inversion.
- iii) The Leading-Tone Diminished Seventh Chord of g minor, harmonic form, in root position.
- iv) The Supertonic Triad of A flat Major, in first inversion.
- v) The Submediant Triad of e minor, in second inversion.

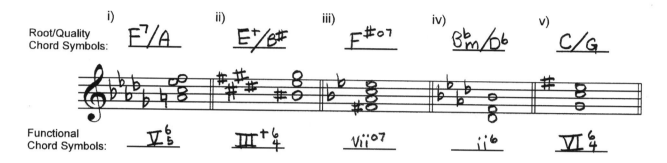

b) For each of the following chords: Name the Major key. Write the Functional Chord Symbol below the staff.

c) Write the following seventh chords of the Functional Chord Symbols. Use accidentals. Use half notes.

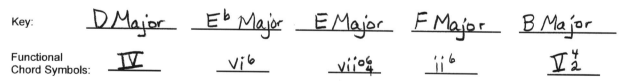

3. a) Add bar lines to complete each of the following rhythms.

b) Add the correct Time Signature below the brackets for each of the following measures.

c) Add rests below the brackets to complete the following measures.

d) Circle TRUE or FALSE for each of the following statements.

TRUE or (FALSE) A Whole Rest fills ANY measure in Simple Time with NO exceptions.

TRUE or (FALSE) A Dotted Whole Rest fills ANY measure in Compound Time.

(TRUE) or FALSE: A Whole Rest receives 2 beats in 3/2 time when a half note value is on beat 3.

TRUE or (FALSE) A Dotted Quarter Rest equals 3 Dotted Eighth Notes.

(TRUE) or FALSE: A Breve Rest fills a measure with silence in 4/2 Time.

4. a) The following melody is written for English Horn in F. Name the key in which it is written.
        Transpose it to concert pitch, using the correct Key Signature. Name the new key.

Key: _A Major_

Key: _D Major_

    b) Name the key of the following melody. Transpose it down a minor 2. Use a Key Signature and any
        necessary accidentals. Name the new key. For each melody, write the Root/Quality Chord
        Symbols (in root position) on strong beat 1 above each measure.

Key: _f minor_

Key: _e minor_

5. The following passage is written in open score for string quartet. Name the four instruments (do not
    use abbreviations). Rewrite the open score into short score.

6. a) Write the following scales, ascending and descending. Use a Key Signature and any necessary accidentals. Use whole notes.

i) F sharp minor, melodic form, from Submediant to Submediant in the Bass Clef.

10

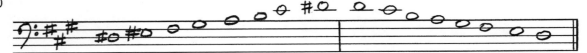

ii) G flat Major scale, from Supertonic to Supertonic in the Alto Clef.

iii) G sharp minor, harmonic form, from Mediant to Mediant in the Tenor Clef.

iv) Enharmonic Relative minor, natural form, of C sharp Major in the Treble Clef.

v) Phrygian mode starting on F sharp in the Bass Clef. Use any standard notation.

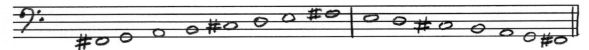

vi) Lydian mode starting on B flat in the Treble Clef. Use any standard notation.

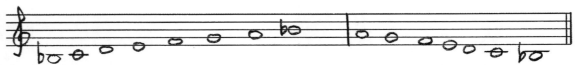

b) Name the following scales as Major Pentatonic, minor Pentatonic, Whole Tone, Blues or Octatonic.

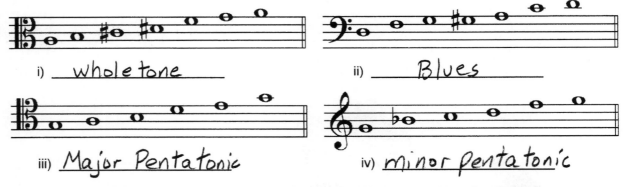

i) __whole tone__

ii) __Blues__

iii) __Major Pentatonic__

iv) __minor pentatonic__

7. a) Name the key of the melodic opening. Write the Time Signature on the music below the bracket.
    b) Compose an Answer Phrase to create a Contrasting Period, ending on a stable scale degree.
    c) Draw a phrase mark over each phrase. d) Name the type of each cadence (Authentic or Half).

Key: b minor   Cadence: Half

Cadence: Authentic

8. For each of the following melodies: a) Name the key.
    b) Write a cadence in Keyboard Style below the bracketed notes.
    c) Label the chords using Functional Chord Symbols.
    d) Name the type of cadence (Authentic, Half or Plagal).

Key: Db Major   Cadence: Plagal

Key: b minor   Cadence: Half

Ultimate Music Theory
Level 8 Theory Exam

9. a) Identify the work to which each of the following statements applies by writing the appropriate letter (**A**, **B**, **C**, **D** or **E**) in the space before each statement.

10

              A - *Ordo Vitutum*
              B - *Sumer Is Icumen In* ("Reading Rota")
              C - *El grillo*
              D - Javanese gamelan "Kaboran (Gamelan Prawa)"
              E - "Evening Raga: Bhopali"

C   This piece uses word painting, connecting the text with the music.

D   Classical overture piece (based on sléndro scale), played at the Shadow Puppet Show.

B   This anonymous 13th Century Round has a bass ostinato pattern.

D   Performed by an ensemble of mostly tuned percussion instruments including metallophones.

E   Indian classical music with rhythmic cycles and melodic improvisation.

A   This Medieval plainchant is in monophonic texture.

B   This canon is in polyphonic texture written for six voices *a cappella*.

E   The Performing Forces used in this piece are the Sitar, Tabla and Tanpoora.

A   This morality play was composed by Hildegard von Bingen

C   This *frottola* composed by Josquin des Prez begins using homorhythmic texture.

b) Match each musical term or sign with the English definition. (Not all definitions will be used.)

Term		Definition
vite	c	a) playful
mit Ausdruck	e	b) moderate, moderately
scherzando	a	c) fast
langsam	l	d) moving
cédez	j	e) with expression
largamente	k	f) with fire
mässig	b	g) in a singing style
bewegt	d	h) dying, fading away
con fuoco	f	i) sad
dolente	i	j) yield; hold the tempo back
cantabile	g	k) broadly
		l) slow, slowly

10. Analyze the excerpt of the Gigue by G. F. Handel (1685 - 1759) by answering the questions below.

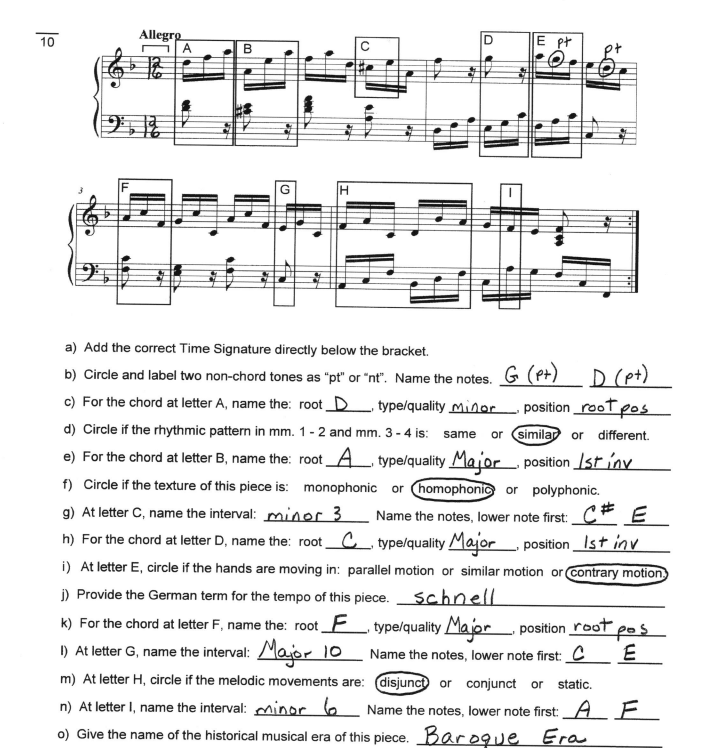

a) Add the correct Time Signature directly below the bracket.

b) Circle and label two non-chord tones as "pt" or "nt". Name the notes. <u>G (pt)   D (pt)</u>

c) For the chord at letter A, name the: root <u>D</u>, type/quality <u>minor</u>, position <u>root pos</u>

d) Circle if the rhythmic pattern in mm. 1 - 2 and mm. 3 - 4 is: same   or   (similar)   or   different.

e) For the chord at letter B, name the: root <u>A</u>, type/quality <u>Major</u>, position <u>1st inv</u>

f) Circle if the texture of this piece is: monophonic   or   (homophonic)   or   polyphonic.

g) At letter C, name the interval: <u>minor 3</u>   Name the notes, lower note first: <u>C♯   E</u>

h) For the chord at letter D, name the: root <u>C</u>, type/quality <u>Major</u>, position <u>1st inv</u>

i) At letter E, circle if the hands are moving in: parallel motion   or   similar motion   or   (contrary motion.)

j) Provide the German term for the tempo of this piece. <u>schnell</u>

k) For the chord at letter F, name the: root <u>F</u>, type/quality <u>Major</u>, position <u>root pos</u>

l) At letter G, name the interval: <u>Major 10</u>   Name the notes, lower note first: <u>C   E</u>

m) At letter H, circle if the melodic movements are: (disjunct)   or   conjunct   or   static.

n) At letter I, name the interval: <u>minor 6</u>   Name the notes, lower note first: <u>A   F</u>

o) Give the name of the historical musical era of this piece. <u>Baroque Era</u>

Ultimate Music Theory Certificate

has successfully completed all the requirements of the

Music Theory Level 8

Music Teacher   _Date_

Enriching Lives Through Music Education